KEEP ON WRITING!

From Creative Writer to Professional Writer

André Jute

DStJT

WN

ISBN 0 946537 65 8

A catalogue record for this book is available from the British Library

Set in 11/12.5pt Sabon by XL Publishing Services, Nairn
Printed in Great Britain by Billing & Son, Worcester
for David St John Thomas Publishers
PO Box 4, Nairn, Scotland IV12 4HU

CONTENTS

1
THE NEVER-COMPLEAT WRITER
UNEQUALLY STAGED
DEVELOPMENT

THE true novice writer can choose from a plethora of
advice, including my own in the companion book to this
one, *Start Writing Today!* The established author can call
his* agent or publisher or even other writers for advice –
though most don't, preferring to make mistakes rather than
appear ignorant. But the creative writer in between – the one
who has survived the initial major effort of perseverance and
frustration of the first book and is now trying to turn himself
into a professional author – is not so lucky. He has outgrown
the basic advice so freely available but doesn't yet have the
contacts to obtain expert counsel; furthermore, because of
the nature of the creative process, he will often not know
precisely which problem he faces and will therefore be unable
to formulate a useful question. Subliminally he understands
that the questions he must face have moved onto a different
plane from those he met and solved as a novice but, unable to
articulate the dimensions and particulars of his new difficulties, he suffers in silence and probably drops out of the
profession before truly establishing himself. One big
commercial publisher with a background in a small literary
house reckons that half of those who write no more after
publishing one or two books drop out because the books

---

*He includes She throughout. Certainly I believe God is a woman and that we live
in a matriarchy but that has nothing to do with the conventions of comprehensible,
flowing writing.

failed – that is, the rewards were too small for the writer rather than the publisher, because no publisher will publish your first book unless he believes well enough in your potential to give you more than two chances – but the other half 'just loses interest in writing, for all the wrong reasons'.

The published writers who drop out make up only the visible tip of the iceberg. Behind them stands a veritable army of unpublished writers who have proven they have the skill to finish a book but then do not know how to take the next step to becoming professionals. It is difficult to conceive of another profession in which such wilful waste is so blithely condoned. That, in part, is why I wrote this book, because I abhor waste, and waste of talent above all. Also, less altruistically, I read faster than good new books are published, and should like to be entertained and informed by the good books you will write once you get over the 'hump' between being a dedicated amateur and becoming a regular professional.

Is this book for you?   If you have written and *fully* cut and revised a full-length work of creative fiction or non-fiction or drama, if you are circulating it to publishers or producers, if you have another 'in the drawer' awaiting cutting and rewriting, and if you are already working on a third, you are my ideal reader. Never mind how frustrating your difficulties are, they are unique only in your context; in their general form I or writers known to me have suffered from the same problems and can help you with either specific solutions or, better still, with a frame of mind that makes it easier for you to find a cure for yourself. If you are this writer, you have proven you possess that will to write and to write well and to be published, that dogged persistence which more than any other characteristic distinguishes the professional writer. It is true that a writer needs much more than this to succeed but without perseverance all your talent, learned skill and acquired outlook are worthless.

You will get best value from this book if you have completed at least one full-length creative work, so that you may share our common faiths and will have close acquaintance with a writer's tribulations and frustrations. It is true

8

that the quick and the clever might use this book as a compendium of awful warnings and quick fixes but that would be to defeat its purpose. My working style – it really isn't grand enough to be called 'a method' – is to guide you towards a way of thinking that helps you solve even unique problems; no book could contain all specific problems and even if it could it would require updating every time a new problem popped up, which would be tiresome for both of us and far less productive for you. My instructional mode virtually requires, if it is to be effective, that you discover the problem on your own and gain familiarity with its aspects by struggling with it yourself; in the same way, carpenters who will work mainly with machine tools are trained with hand tools so that they can become familiar with the woods they will work in. If you have solved a problem or two yourself, without my help, so much the better, because you will instantly see the logic of the solutions in this book, and ways in which to adapt them to your own work.

The writer who has had a book or two published and now is in the slough of despond is not a special case: it happens to a lot of writers, especially the ones who got lucky without too much hard graft. The pain is worse if they are very talented and everyone, including themselves, knows they have many more books in them but just can't get a good hold on the next one. Somehow it seems degrading for a writer whose name has been up in lights – well, at least favourably reviewed in the *New York Times Book Review* and the (London)*Times Literary Supplement* – to be forced to seek help. I was in this plight after my third book, and there was nothing on my library's shelves of any use to that particular circumstance. Twenty books later I still remember that time with a literal shudder and more than a little bitterness; it was a far more frightening experience than being shot at. Fortunately I had agents and editors and publishers to help me, and the advantage of a personality which responds positively to challenge and adversity, but agents and editors have less and less time to be helpful to writers and the majority of writers are sensitive and unaggressive people. This book will, I hope, help all these nice folk as well as the hardball players.

Shared assumptions   Certain basic attitudes that are acquired in the creation of a full-length creative work and the process of publishing it will in this book be taken as axiomatic and presumed to be held in common with you, the reader. Where they are made explicit, low-level detail will be left out because the purpose will be a quick refresher of something you already know, or the approach will be from one of the less obvious tangents in order to illuminate a more – sometimes much more – advanced aspect of a problem than one would find in a book for true novices. For the genuine basics, I refer you to John Braine's *Writing a Novel*, Brenda Ueland's *So You Want to Write*, and my own *Start Writing Today!*, to which this book is a direct, advanced continuation – the two books were conceived as a set to serve writers at various stages in their careers. If you are a thriller-writer, my *Writing a Thriller* is aimed specifically at taking the thriller-writer from his first writing urges through to publication of his first book, and from there you can pick up the thread here.

These are the minimum assumptions I hold axiomatic for writers and which will therefore not in this book be defended or comprehensively explained, but *will* underlie everything we discuss:

Perseverance. We have already touched on this most desirable of personal characteristics for a writer. Good books are not written but rewritten, great books are persistent rewrites of rewrites. Perseverance in writing and in all your other professional relationships is a prerequisite for every writer and a characteristic publishers and editors look out for keenly. Any editor who comes into the business thinking that writing a book is easy is soon disabused of that notion. He comes across an alarming number of people he knows to be bright and industrious who fail to finish books on which the same editor may well have persuaded his publisher to make a cash advance, a factor which speeds up the editor's learning process rather sharply; smart editors and publishers are the ones who learn soonest to look out for the writer with persistence. I well remember Bernard Sher-Cliff, when he was editor-in-chief of Warner Books in New York, coming to visit me in Cambridge, England, after buying my first novel.

Virtually the moment the small talk was over he settled into what had every appearance of an interrogator's practised routine: he wanted to know about my work habits, what exercise I took and how regularly, whether I had a strict working routine, whether I was in good health. He was obviously taken aback when he heard I rose at ten in the morning when my wife brought me breakfast in bed. But he brightened when he discovered I always worked until at least midnight and often until two in the morning. When I mentioned this extraordinary performance to my agent, Peter Grose, I was told to look to the general direction of the questions, which were all aimed at discovering whether I would stick to the job in hand, finish the book on my typewriter, and the next, and the next, meanwhile doing all the necessary rewrites and absorbing all the small and large blows apparently inseparable from the life of an author. Peter added that he himself had already been impressed by the speed, good cheer and thoroughness with which I did the rewrite he had asked for on another book.

The primacy of character over plot, event, theme, concept, action, beautiful writing, *everything*, is the second assumption. It is best learned the hard way, in writing your own work and dissecting reasons why it fails, but here we will assume that you have broken through that particular painful threshold and agree with me not only on the primacy of character in space and weight but also that all good things flow from proper characterisation – and most bad things follow inexorably from failing to control your characters. If you are not familiar with the formal and practical (even pragmatic) and commercial arguments for this belief, you should review them in *Start Writing Today!*, *Writing a Thriller*, or in the anthologised chapter from the latter in the 1989 edition of *Novel & Short Story Writer's Market,* which is available from the stacks of your library. It is impossible to stress the importance of character too much – you should know it not only in your gut from hard experience but also in your head from calculated reasoning. Character, besides being the most deeply satisfying of a writer's creations, is also money in the bank. Forgive me for stressing a point so obvious, but every time I write on this subject letters arrive even from well-published writers expressing their heartfelt gratitude for explaining something they seem to think is new – but which obviously they already knew and accepted deep in their subconscious before they read me because otherwise they would neither be published nor grasp the concept so readily. Note that in every book there is character, even in a how-to book like this one, where you and I are the characters: you have already formed an opinion about me from the style and approach.

The third important assumption is that we are engaged in a craft or a profession rather than primarily in an art, and that we have to be craftsmen and professionals before we become artists. Don't forget this, especially in those places where this book unavoidably sounds like Norman Vincent Peale on Creative Writing. If you do not believe that you must master the technique of the craft before you can produce even competent work, never mind art, we have come to a parting of the ways already; even the most optimistic of editors, who lives in expectation of discovering a genius, does not believe in the writer so talented that he can scorn craft and technique. The word 'creative' in our sense does not distinguish art from the rest but is merely a convenient label for a certain class of written content. The writing we are concerned with is not strictly technical matter; it is made difficult by the requirement for imaginative input; it is judged by more and other criteria than clarity of content; and it is not by its nature excluded from the possibility of becoming art. This book provides techniques for overcoming the psychological and technical barriers the 'requirement for imaginative input' places in the writer's path. Harnessing, controlling and guiding your imagination is an entirely professional necessity for a writer, far different from posing around in black polo necks (mine are cotton and imported from Australia), spouting off about 'creativity' and 'suffering for your art'. This is not however either to scorn or limit your sensibilities and ambition, both of which are taken for granted, but to save you unnecessary effort. My definition of art – the judgement of history – is in fact wider than is currently fashionable. Certainly I would class as art *Zen and the Art of Motorcycle Maintenance* or any writing by the delightful L.J.K. Setright on matters automobile precisely because these creators not only have something to say but have mastered the craft and technique of communicating their material most effectively and affectively. You cannot touch people emotively – another good definition of art – if you are not in command of your mode of expression. And, once you have mastered craft and technique, concern about 'art' is unnecessary and even counterproductive, something you can safely leave to those without any creative talent at all, because *your* art has become a self-tending organism fed by the unique style that comes with mastery of technique.

Using this book It follows from our final assumption that you should judge this book by the benefits it brings to your own work. The best way to use it is to read it right through so that you can find your way around the various chapters and then to keep it on your desk until you hit trouble in your own work, when you should refer via the chapter-heads or the index to the relevant sections.

Nothing in this book is carved on stone, except the three basic assumptions above, without which we cannot have a meeting of minds. Everything else is my own opinion and nothing more. It was formed from personal experience gathered in the writing of more than twenty books and a dozen full-length items for other media, from the descriptions of other writers (and sometimes other artists because I have long been interested in the motivation of all kinds of creators), from talking to editors and managerial and marketing people at the thirty-odd publishers I deal with in a dozen countries. Such depth of experience may be a recommendation – or it may hide the fact that we are so accustomed to the trees cutting off our view that we can no longer perceive the forest! It would be intellectually satisfying to know in each instance why some piece of advice works but this is not a theoretical book and I have therefore included effective solutions even when their mechanism is unknown or seems illogical. It is however a personal book – it could hardly be anything else, given the nature of our craft – and I have therefore included only what works for me or another writer whose judgement I trust. It follows that when something does not work for you, it is my fault and not yours; it also follows that your own solution, given only that it works at least as well as mine, is always the better choice for your own work, for psychological reasons as much as practical.

Unless you're a very slow writer you should not need this book for more than two or three years. Writing is itself a learning experience. At the beginning of your career, you should have three or four books in various stages of conception, writing, lying fallow, and rewriting, and in these you will run into enough problems of the kind canvassed in these pages to allow you, with the help of the solutions we discuss, to develop your own methods and frames of mind for meeting and beating troubles. It is not the specific solution described that is most useful to you, however grateful you may be at that moment for the quick fix which allows you to keep working, but the confidence of knowing most problems are not insoluble, that almost all can be solved by the simplest means, and that the majority are avoidable through proper work-methods. Throw this book away, or give it to another writer, the first time you develop a better solution to any problem than the one described here, even if there are still plenty of solutions you haven't used. Remember, the more you write, the better your chances of improving your writing. I should be delighted if, after reading this book through, you never have to open it again but, sadly, that is not a realistic expectation. However, keep in mind that your purpose is not to learn *about* writing better but to learn *to write better*. The sooner you learn to adapt the solutions here quite out of recognition, the sooner you will develop that independent frame of mind which allows you to overcome new difficulties and carry on working regardless. I can't increase your talent but I can, with your help, give you the confidence that translates to productivity that translates to more confidence that translates to more productivity; a beneficial circle. Once they achieve this confidence, most writers on the 'hump' need only a small push to turn into self-generating dynamos.

2
CREATING AN OMNI-TOOL
YOUR IDEAL READER

THE novice writer's burning desire to write provides its own lamp oil because the subject comes to him together with the conviction that he should write about it. There may be enough oil to light a second book and more rarely, according to some publishers hardly ever, even enough for a third book. Then burnout. The writer lapses from the faith altogether or falls into a slough of despond. His work, if he manages to create any, is of inferior quality to the standard he has already set. This is a lot more common than appears to the cursory glance. Part of the problem is hidden behind unproven assumptions which have crept into publishers' 'received wisdom', such as that everyone has one book in him, which implies that we're all very lucky when an author serendipitously produces a readable second book. Another easy assumption is that a non-fiction writer has exhausted his store of knowledge in his first book and that it is therefore foolish to expect a second book from him. Of course there are writers who truly have only one book in them, for instance the serious hobbyist orchid-breeder who spends half a lifetime creating an encyclopedic volume on his subject and then has nothing more to say, or the man who knows all there is to know about witch burnings in his twee village in the back of beyond. But they are the exception.

In truth the archetypal one-book writer is Barbara Cartland, who has written over five hundred volumes flogging her single theme, that chastity is repaid by marriage to Mr Right. But, even admitting that she does not have the major concern of most other writers, that of finding an overall theme for her new book, consider a few of her other problems. Where does she get fresh names for her characters? Fresh differentiation for her characters? Fresh settings of geography and milieu? Fresh plot, with a full quota of engrossing and illuminating events? The majority of readers of this book are probably serious-minded authors who are likely to be offended by the choice of Barbara Cartland as an example. I make no apology: she is the ideal choice to illustrate an important point, contained in the conjunction of her gigantic output with the well-publicised regularity of her working routine: it gets easier each time you start a new book, until eventually you are – almost – on auto-pilot.

For the absolute novice writing a first or a second book in a flush of enthusiasm and for the veteran writing his fiftieth it is easy; for everyone in between it is painful to some degree or another. The most dangerous point of the transition from novice to veteran lies at the beginning.

It is probably true that most of us will never write so many books or become so professional that the process of starting a new one becomes automatic and therefore completely painless, as in the case of Anthony Trollope who if he finished one book at 4.45pm would immediately start writing the next one because his writing-time was not over until 5pm! But after thirty-plus novels, non-fiction books, films and plays, I can start a new book with the minimum and sometimes no notes, and often within a month of the time I had planned to start it, and many less experienced but better disciplined authors improve on that. That surely is a happier condition than after my third book when nearly two years passed in frustrated idleness for lack of direction-giving methodology – or simple tricks of the trade – for finding a new theme.

At this point, before you start worrying that you will never discover another theme to match your first one or two, it is worth bringing out into the open the subconscious mechanism by which those themes arose. In the process, and after considering some external factors that never occur to the novice but that the professional cannot afford to ignore, we will construct a tool, which I imagine as a set of calipers with emotions. You can measure all aspects of your work against this tool – starting with your new theme, which I will help you discover in the next chapter.

YOUR IDEAL READER

Most of us became writers because we were readers first. We ran out of books we liked to read and therefore took to writing them. A few of us became writers because we had some specialist knowledge that drew a publisher's attention and we so liked the experience of creating something lasting that we wanted to repeat it. That's how I came to write non-fiction after establishing myself as a novelist, because a publisher thought the Bentley I was rebuilding plus my experience as a motor racer and chassis developer would make a good base for a book on designing and building special cars. I liked the change of pace and the boost of getting letters from absolute strangers one has helped and I therefore cast around for other fields in which I would have something useful to contribute.

Harlotry and helotry   Whatever the origins of your writing career, you probably write first of all to please yourself. That's good, because writing 'for a market' in which you can't bear to read your competition will bring you nothing but pain and disappointment and poverty. The great and noteworthy thing about Barbara Cartland, the aspect of her work which has made her a perennial bestseller, is that she believes fervently not only in her moral message (which is her own business) but in all its implications; her sincerity is obvious to her readers and brings them back for more in a way her imitators cannot match because they lack the True Faith. It is not the legendary Cartland trashiness that sells but her honest-to-goodness, perfectly innocent belief in the rightness of her message. She succeeds because she writes precisely what she wants to read and is therefore her own fiercest critic. Those authors who falsely concluded that trash sells and tried to pay the bills by imitating Dame Barbara have all ended up on the dole queue. Serves them right for being so stupid as not to understand that, *in her own terms,* Barbara Cartland serves up a quality product.

The snake   Unfortunately, Barbara Cartland's is the only part of the book-reading spectrum, except perhaps for the pornographer's, which still lives in the unblinking innocence of Eden. The rest of us have been cast out into the wilderness of Sophistication.

Now, if your dream is to write for Mills & Boon or Harlequin, don't put this book down just because I sneer at La Cartland. Let this be your first lesson in growing a thick skin against 'the shit endemic to a life in the arts' (an apt phrase all writers must thank William Goldman for): plenty of intellectual snobs, including some in editorial departments whose colleagues just down the hall are in the fertiliser business, will sneer at you. Let them – they'll still have overdrafts when you own the bank.

The routines, techniques and trade tips in this book make no moral distinction whatsoever between the writer of trashy romances, the chronicler of the bogus high-life, and the creator of deeply 'relevant' kitchen sink novels – see, I sneer equally at the pretensions of the hyper-sophisticated. The best test of a writer's success is publication, better still repeated publication, which implies that he services a market of readers because otherwise publishers would eschew his work. And the techniques of improving your communication with readers are essentially the same whether those readers are sophisticated or naive, and equally the same for all writers including the flashily artistic, the solid craftsman storyteller, the meticulous biographer, the lively illuminator of history, the modest journeyman writer and the humble spinner of solace for lonely-heart secretaries.

Depths and levels   Unfortunately, while the techniques may be the same for every writer, whatever his level of sophistication or his subject or genre, the level of application is not the same but is differentiated by the expectations of the writer's readers and by the literary conventions they are familiar with and willing to accept. This is best illustrated with two examples.

18

A lady I know has a first class honours degree in Romance languages from one of the better British universities, which, for American readers, is probably as good as a Ph.D. in an obscure subject from an Ivy League college. But she likes reading historical romances for relaxation, so that is what she writes. Her novels are many steps up the ladder from the Cartland School of Perpetual Innocence, but a comparison between her academic writings in her speciality and her equally professional writing for entertainment shows simpler sentence structures in the latter, a much more comprehensible and attractive vocabulary even when one makes allowance for the jargon expected in academic technical writing, and greater patience in explication and development in the fiction. The novels are published under another name and one suspects many of her academic colleagues who are unaware of her other career would, from the internal evidence of the writing alone, fail to identify her as the creator of the fiction – whereas they could probably identify her as the author of an academic paper from reading only a few paragraphs. When taxed with this as a kind of hypocrisy, she replies, 'No, it is what is expected by readers. That is the style I like to read romances in, not 'written down' but the writer must absolutely not put difficulties in my path just to show how clever she is, or because she's too lazy to rewrite a paragraph. As for my professional work, I hate to be treated by other writers like some first-year student who hasn't yet found the library, so I do unto my colleagues as I should like them to do unto me.'

Contrast this with a writer with a large claque among the literarily ultra-sophisticated, and perfectly respectable sales to what his wife, a very aware literary agent, considers to be mainly a campus/academic readership. According to her she encourages him to 'let all that expensive Oxbridge literary prejudice hang out. It doesn't really matter what he says, as long as he doesn't buck the predominantly-left politics most intellectuals still cling to. What they really like is to see the gears meshing. If you're going to be a serious writer, you should make it easy for your readers to make formal analyses of your work in the currently-favoured mode. Be the first writer to be written up by whoever comes after the post-structuralists and I can get you a tidy advance for your next book... Of course none of this has anything to do with the books people in the popular market want to read. Much as we may regret it, the two markets have split for good.'

It is quite obvious that these two writers, who have much in common as people, who move in the same circle and share many friends and interests, write differently for different groups of readers, and that they assume their readers have different expectations of them. A point immediately worth noting is that the first writer, who gets good reviews in the heavies for her historical romances even though the critics are the last people on her mind when she writes, operates under stricter constrictions of quality control: comprehensibility and the communication of sometimes complicated historical constructs to the least sophisticated of her readers are her minimum requirements and these impose the maximum burdens on the writer. The second writer, who is frankly and exultantly in the business of creating literary puzzles for their own sake and for the delectation of the same people who will review his book in the heavies, has an easier job because there is no restraint on either his inventiveness or his method (except the modest hypocrisy that he must demonstrate acceptable politics). He is *expected* to be incomprehensible to all but a small self-selecting audience; as he himself puts it, 'If they can't follow me, that's because they're stupid.'

Very few of the rest of us can afford the arrogance of such a statement – which perhaps explains why the majority of writers of and for the literary intelligentsia have tenured and richly rewarded academic jobs – but equally not many of us possess the discipline of the romance writer who has consistently over nearly twenty books kept two writing styles compartmentalised. Most writers have one painfully acquired and honed style for all occasions because they write for only one audience, themselves. We shall return in a moment to why you should give more thought to your readers than merely to define them as someone like yourself, but first it is worth considering whether there is any sense in making the large effort required to adapt your style to more than one audience or to a larger audience.

The educated village? We hear much about the global village but its reality is more pertinent to the balance sheets of multinational media tycoons, and to the EEC bureaucracy in Brussels, than evident to the writer – even in English, the most commonly understood language in the world. (There are more Russians who speak English than the entire population of the British Isles, and several times as many Chinese). Forget the obvious cultural differences as the time-zones move around the world; there are simply too many of them for you ever to take them all into account. Forget vernacular differences: the writer either has the local rhythm and slang or he has not, and copy editors can take care of variant usage in technical terms between the UK and USA. Just consider this: an American and an Englishman read to a different cadence and one must assume that their comprehension is attuned, by usage and expectation, each to his own cadence. There are British writers who become scathing about books by American writers because, it appears on questioning, they feel the American author is deliberately insulting their intelligence; if you try to pin them down, they can point to such objective features as simplified sentence structures, uncomplicated and fully- or over-explicated plots, and a lot of other detail that is equally unconvincing or conclusive, depending on where you stand. They do not comprehend that an American writer does not operate in a British environment but in his own. This is not a version of cultural imperialism but plain ignorance. The mutual incomprehension also works in reverse, with Americans complaining that British authors tend to make things difficult for the reader from sheer perversity or, worse, lack of care, by long, complicated sentences, a love of word variation for its own sake, and plots or subplots that go nowhere. A common American complaint from unsophisticated readers about Le Carré, a leading British novelist with big sales in the States, is that 'he is coy, he doesn't come right out and say what he means'. I sympathise with this view, because what the British label as

21

understatement or subtlety is more often than not merely tiresome padding when we should just straightforwardly be told the story. All of which explains why the British writer the Americans love best is the briskly efficient Dick Francis.

This also applies at the other end of the scale. An American how-to book or article in the specialist press always seems tediously comprehensive and unnecessarily explicative to a Britisher, who concludes that Mr Glenn (of *Bicycle Manual* fame) is treating him like a moron who can't work out anything for himself. Conversely, the American who can't find all the nuts and bolts actually illustrated in a British manual concludes that the author 'must have promoted himself an expert because his mother said he could'. This was the verdict of one disgusted American on a British book which had nothing serious amiss except that the publisher optimistically described it as an introduction for laymen. In Britain the word layman describes an enthusiast willing to go to the library and do supplementary research, but in the States it describes a genuine do-it-yourselfer who may or may not have a college degree but is equally likely not to know where the library is and consequently needs the full answer right there on one page – and has been accustomed by his own publishers to getting it. There are exceptions. The success of the exemplary Haynes automobile manuals, published from the British countryside at Yeovil, is very probably due to their taking the ultra-thorough American nuts-and-bolts approach to every single book they do. Several of the handful of really readable grubby-bits writers are British but most of these have, like David Vizard, long since emigrated to the States.

Differences go deeper than that. To the educated European, it is perfectly natural that writing on technical matters should share literary intent. My book on the design of automobiles, *Designing and Building Special Cars*, is at least as well written as any of my novels and ranges over metaphysical matters beyond mere technicalities where it seems meet. L.J.K. Setright has turned consideration of automobile antecedents into most readable and entertaining social history. Primo Levi's scientific work is widely considered literature; so are the writings of a whole bunch of writers on mental health whose specific theories have long since been partially or wholly discredited (Freud, Adler, Jung, Laing, et al). My automobile book was a bestseller for me in Europe but I was told it would have done better in the States if I had concentrated more on the hotrodding aspect at the expense of the 'theory and justification'. When the leading American automobile magazine extended a regular column to Mr Setright, who is as English as only a true eccentric can be, one could almost see them patting themselves on the back in congratulation at their daring in giving so 'literary' an automobile writer a go. Shortly after this experiment was proved a success, those considerable numbers of their staff capable of turning a striking phrase suddenly started lashing out and an always knowledgeable magazine instantly became readable for the pleasure of the prose as well, prose which at times was bitchier even than the fashion or literary press. This process has nothing to do with an American inferiority complex but rather with what the editors thought their readers expected of them. It is not difficult to find sophisticated Americans who are baffled by the regard in which Levi is held in Europe, and even more baffled by my explanation that he stands in the direct line of Hume, Carlyle, and Rousseau, all of whom the British, French and Germans read as literature. The stumbling-block is that the Americans have a long history of receiving their literary culture in the form of pre-digested public performances such as Emerson's self-improvement lectures and Dickens' histrionic readings. These functions are now performed by writers going on the telechat tour. The British do not have this heritage of the lecture tour but did routinely read novels and much more serious books aloud in groups in country houses and parsonages. It is also noticeable that the moment a guru is professionally discredited sales of his books fall off in the States no matter how amusingly he writes, which is not invariably true in Europe.

One final extreme example. I'm all in favour of simple computer manuals, and indeed wrote a book about a particular computer, the Epson PX-8, when I discovered that just reading through the manuals took me forty-three hours. I calculated the average business user could not afford that amount of time, especially if instead he could buy a (high royalty, expensive) quick guide which would give him results in an hour, and which could be written from my own existing operating notes. When I sent a copy of this book to an American publisher as an example of my neddy-style, it came straight back with an example of what *he* considered a suitable style of writing for American executives. When I complained that I could not write about the selection of retail locations as if for eight-year-olds, he insisted that was the proper level. The deal fell through. This may be a case of a publisher having contempt for his market (this one has since fallen into financial difficulties and been taken over) but I mention it to illustrate that even honest differences of opinion tend to widen the cultural gap rather than narrow it even between two such closely allied cultures as the British (which this publisher wrongly assumed me to be) and the American.

For the American writer in general, with his huge home market, it is probably neither necessary nor possible to consider the other English-speaking markets and to learn to cater for them. For the serious American writer, especially of fiction and those very important higher branches of creative non-fiction such as biography, history, political and current affairs, it is, at least in my opinion, necessary to consider the expectations and prejudices of the kissing cousins across the water, both as to content and expression. The fast way to learn is to live in Europe for a while, and even sojourns in Canada and Australia, where the cultures are Anglo-American hybrids, are often seminal experiences for American writers. At least you must read their current literature in your field, from which you will be able to deduce much.

The British writer of every class *must* consider the biggest market for English-language books in the world, the USA. There is no escaping it. I am not advocating that you turn your style into a travesty of mid-Atlantic cabin-speak but simply that you do not commit stupidities such as caught my eye in a recent novel: the writer, to emphasise the Britishness of a character, exaggerated precisely those facets of English writing which the Americans most abhor – when it was clear he could have chosen other facets more easily accessible to a very definite, very large potential group of readers. Living in the States is an eye-opener but at least the British writer should read widely among the American writers.

Obviously there are exceptions. What I have said so far may be perfectly all right for me, a cosmopolitan writer without discernible roots whose first novel was published simultaneously in New York, London and Melbourne, and whose themes are deliberately selected in the hope that they will have universal appeal. But, at the other end of this spectrum, we all know writers whose very strength is their rootedness in a region, even a city or a village, or in an ethnic group or a social class or even in their gender; these writers must therefore take the greatest care not to dilute the impact of their work when they try to make it more accessible to a wider audience. However, the best of even the most rooted writers – Herriot (the vet with the talent for projecting the Yorkshire Dales), Malamud, Bunyan, Chaucer and Potok immediately spring to mind – have universal appeal because their linguistic simplicity transcends time and place. Be careful that regional or ethnic or historical accent does not become an excuse rather than a reason for not reaching out to a wider audience. Need I say in a book for professional writers that dialect writing, defined as rendering ethnic or class or regional accents phonetically in English for extended passages, is utterly unacceptable unless your name happens to be Leo Q Rosten? He is chosen *because Mr Rosten does not actually write dialect* though his sleight of hand is to give every appearance of doing so; there is a lovely introduction to the collected *Kaplan* stories in which he generously explains how he achieves his effect and, more to the point for the rest of us who might be tempted but do not have his unique ear, demolishes the possibility of truly duplicating the accent of dialect in anything approaching comprehensible form, or of its use in more than brief passages.

Such differences of expectation, of what people are used to and comfortable with, exist not only between nations but within them. This is not the place to describe them, socio-economic class by sub-class, even if I knew them. They're your readers and you should be aware of their expectations. This is less troublesome than it might seem, especially for those of us who write what we already read much of, but if you insist on writing 'for a market' you must first immerse yourself in that market. At the very least you should read the same newspapers and watch the same television shows as your intended audience, and talk to many to discover their dreams and aspirations. Better still, live among them for an extended period.

All these national differences and intra-national differences are a good reason for adapting your style to be accessible to more readers. They are also a valid qualifier to the concept of the ideal reader, which we are now ready to define, starting with what he is not.

Statistics and other lies   It is well known that most books are sold to women, or borrowed from libraries by women, whether for themselves or for their men. It is also a truly irrelevant 'fact' for any writer.

Publishers without any competence in statistics discovered this 'fact', initiated a wave of 'woman's fiction' which is just now running out of energy, and installed a lot of women in important editorial and managerial positions, not before time but for all the wrong reasons. Many of these women now justify their jobs by perpetuating an entirely artificial sexual separation of book buyers and borrowers, abetted by a bunch of male editors who are protecting their jobs by promoting all kinds of specialist male categories which no one can prove exists. There is a market for 'women's books' – and it consists of lesbian literature, so-called feminist classics and books on women's liberation which no one has actually proved men do not read too; it is a specialist market well served by publishers such as London's Virago but no place for the big commercial battalions. Many writers are deeply sceptical of the 'marketing strategies' of the big publishers.

Andrew McCoy's realistic stories of people in violent places, a thriller genre known in the trade as 'male-oriented action adventure', increased their sales steadily in Secker & Warburg hardcover and Grafton paperback editions right through the 1980s – a decade when publishing concentrated on women's fiction and family sagas. But Mr McCoy is not impressed by reports that a whole plague of editors are now 'actively seeking male-oriented series fiction for the first time since 1979'. He says, 'These publishing fads have very little to do with readers. I have never seen a guy with muscles buy any of my so-called male-oriented books, but plenty of little old ladies, housewives, young women, and a few fellows who would drop dead if a crocodile smiled at them. We are told ninety-eight per cent of books are bought or borrowed by women. That alone invalidates many subdivisions because substantially more than two per cent of published books are still, by these alleged classifications, supposedly aimed only at men. In the end it always comes down to whether the publisher or an editor with clout personally likes your work, regardless of genre, well enough to lay his company's money on the line and put your book on the shelf in reach of the customer.'

Here's another much-bandied statistic: in any given year, only two per cent of the population will buy a book. You can ignore this one as well, because that two per cent is no longer closely linked to a particular socio-economic class, as it was a couple of generations ago when the middle-class bought most of the books. It's two per cent of everybody, and that two per cent has nothing else significantly in common, so it is no earthly use for the writer seeking an ideal reader.

Listen politely if your publisher starts spouting about what 'research proves'; keep your own counsel and remember that statistics work on a sample of a certain size which brings with it a given 'level of confidence'. These figures of two per cent of this or that might be correct if based on an actual physical count *of every book buyer* ; but if they are based on a very carefully structured sample of 3000 people from the total population they will have a confidence level of five per cent, which means that a nominal 98-2 split could equally be 93-7 or 103 and minus 3. Such statistics aren't worth a chi-square.

27

So you can't write for women, at the beginning of your career you don't know your publisher well enough to define him as your ideal reader, and general market research is no good to you. Not many writers either know how to conduct or can afford purpose-directed research but I was fortunate in having one of my books made the subject of a study by friends in the business.

You can't pitch too high *Reverse Negative* was a novel created specifically as a puzzle for the upper intelligentsia. In form it was a spy thriller but written like an adventure whodunnit with the clues all in place; it pointed to Fourth Man Anthony Blunt while it was still libellous to do so and was, in part, a dare to the authorities (who did indeed confiscate copies of my manuscript and warn me not to publish). This was the novel in which I invented the computer synthesis as a method of telling two stories at once, and of evading the penalty imposed by first-person narratives of being unable convincingly to know what is happening elsewhere. The whole, even in published form, was pretty complicated, but in the penultimate manuscript form, the subject of the test, it was justifiably described as 'ferociously convoluted'. The version published was much simplified, among other reasons in response to the research findings.

The purpose of the test was to determine the potential readership for such a novel. We had two hypotheses, held by various members of the team. The first was that such a novel could only be grasped by the trained and therefore almost inevitably academic mind. This view was held mainly by academics and statisticians. The second was that the progression of clues made it the rightful meat of the middle-class executive relaxing at home after dinner with his favourite reading, detective fiction. This view was held by those of us with experience in business, plus some academics in the marketing and management fields. Never mind how ludicrous our prejudices were only fifteen years ago, concentrate instead on our professionalism: we added a control group, which featured largely in the success of our experiment.

Our sample was made up by finding, at libraries and at

bookshops or through personal acquaintance, seventy-five people who admitted reading fiction. They constituted three groups of twenty-five each. The first group consisted of academics; all had degrees and most had more than one. The second group consisted of senior executives and a number of professional people; most had degrees and many had post-graduate academic or professional qualifications. The third group consisted of nurses, office workers, lower-level teachers, and so on, almost all without university education. This third or control group is included in most empirical research in one form or another not because the researchers expect to learn anything directly from it but as a 'control' on whether circumstances external to the test have influenced the results; in ethical pharmaceutical testing this group is given a placebo rather than the medication under test to monitor whether any improvement measured in the medicated group is not due to psychological rather than chemical causes. Since our test was designed to determine which of two groups of similarly educated but differently employed people would respond best to a particular novel, our control group had a lower level of education but its members were employed in similar surroundings to those of the other two groups, which accounts for the absence of housewives who, in a test conducted today, would certainly be included.

The test itself consisted of giving each participant two-thirds of the manuscript, up to the point where all the clues are present but before the deductions begin. Then we asked our respondents 'whodunnit?'

The results were startling. The academics crashed miserably. The executive types did better but were also disgraced and about half their score was gained by film people who make their living judging popular fiction. The control group of nurses and primary school teachers and secretaries 'won' by a multiple margin.

What this proved was that our hypothetical common denominator, formal education and its close relation, intelligence as measured in IQ tests, had nothing to do with the comprehension of this particular novel.

It turned out on further analysis that our particular bunch

of academics was a skewed sample, because we had selected only those who admitted reading fiction; the general run of academics, who read no fiction at all, would have done even worse. This was a clue.

The executive types did indeed read more fiction than the academics but they weren't all that noticeably into whodunnits, which had been one of the assumptions underlying our hypothesis; in fact they were big on Herman Wouk. Notice that their score was distorted upwards by the inclusion of several film executives who make their living judging fictional material; in a true sample of twenty-five executives there would at most be only one media/entertainment type and that one probably unconcerned with content.

But the individual members of the control group were real readers. Romances, both trashy and quality, got a big cut of their business, Herman Wouk's bestseller was again mentioned significantly. Agatha Christie was not unknown, nor Len Deighton, but it was impossible to conclude that members of the control group were expecially knowledgeable about either the whodunnit or the spy thriller, and certainly not to any extent which would account for their quite extraordinary success in unravelling a purposely difficult crossbreeding of the two genres. We were forced to conclude that any kind of habitual reading, including reading trash, inculcates a familiarity with the conventions of literature across the complete quality spectrum. Come back Dame Barbara, all is forgiven.

No great scientific or statistical claims can be made for our little study. The samples were modest; they were deliberately skewed to get a result at all; both major hypotheses were disproved (that's how science advances, by being forced to create new hypotheses, a process which seems to have escaped some writers in the social sciences); and we lacked the funding to repeat and extend the experiment. But in advertising we often committed tens of millions of dollars on much shakier evidence than this. Besides, this type of research is an art form depending for usable results more on the experience and intuition of the researchers – which is why so many of them specialise – than on statistical verities, so I should like to add one corroborating piece of information: it seems significant support for our main conclusion that film-makers have believed almost from the beginning that 'even trash educates'.

The complete experience is salutary in another respect. It proves that getting your ideal reader wrong need not be disastrous – as long as you pitch too high rather than too low. It also proves the negative face of the same truth, that writing down is unnecessary.

Your own ideal reader We now have a solid base on which to put together your own ideal reader. He reads what you like to read. He is somewhat more intelligent than you, because that is the optimum assumption to safeguard you against writing down. If there is a literary convention he is not familiar with, you have never heard of it either. (That should not however entice you to use rare or unusual conventions or formats for any reason except that your story demands it; the reader stopped by an author to puzzle out which convention is being applied doesn't make a mental note of your clever-ness – he concludes that you are a show-off.) He would like to be able to recommend your book to his kissing cousins on the other side of the Atlantic pond who march to a different drummer; he also has cousins in Canada and Australia.

It would be as well for you to write the specific character-istics of your ideal reader on a sheet of paper to which you can refer for a time and then destroy when it has served its purpose.

Of course my ideal reader shares with yours the generali-ties in the first paragraph of this section but I have given him all my pet hates. Most follow from the generalities. I cannot stand being patronised, especially by intellectual inferiors, so I try never to address my readers in a patronising tone, which is a special form of writing down. Nothing makes me put down a book for good more often than spending ten minutes with an author, say twenty pages, and not having by then discovered in which direction he is taking me. To avoid this happening to my books, each one starts with a bang, no matter how inconvenient it might be to rewrite whole sections and more than once a whole book to place the bang at the beginning. (This gives books of mine that my publishers and I would blush to promote as anything but novels a useful edge in the lucrative thriller market.) You can take it from there: give your ideal reader, as well as a supply of your own most attractive characteristics, a surfeit of your least attractive traits – intolerance, impatience, etc – selected to keep you, the writer, on your toes.

Your ideal reader is still the same measuring device you had as a novice, mildly modified to allow for the realities of a professional writer's world, but he is now much more useful in that he has been brought from the subconscious to the fore of all your cerebrations. His least purpose is to stop you making stupid mistakes by providing a yardstick against which you can measure whatever impresses you – a great idea that only you can see, a piece of fine writing that you love but that doesn't say anything in particular and that would irritate the hell out of you if found in another writer's book. Your ideal reader, carefully crafted, is enough like you to prevent you from straying onto byways where you will get lost, yet he has enough alien influence and exaggeration in his character to provide an abrasive second opinion. He acts as a goad that forces you to extend your talent. He is a friend worth cultivating carefully.

3
WHAT IS LEFT TO SAY:
A CONCEPT SPOTTER'S GUIDE

IT doesn't really matter to the quality of your finished work what you call the parts which make up your writing, or the conventions you use in planning it. In fact, being educated in motivational psychology, economics and business management rather than in literature, I had no need of names for these things until I started writing for other writers and required descriptive labels. You probably have no labels either but it is easier for us to understand each other if we define our terminology in advance.

CONCEPT, THEME, PLOT, EVENT, CHARACTER

Two decades of discussions with publishers, editors and agents have not left me any legacy of widely agreed common names, so let's for the time being use these, which may not be perfect but are simple and easy to remember.

Concept This is the overall point of your book. Here are several concepts suggested by the actions of Mikhail Gorbachev: the tragedy of communism, the failure of socialism, the triumph of goodwill over bureaucracy, that only the strong can set a good example, and no doubt several dozen others you can think up to suit whatever field of writing is your metier. This entire chapter, after these introductory definitions, is about discovering new concepts – and reconditioning old ones as good as new and twice as convincing.

Theme   A theme is a point you wish to make. A number of related themes together make up a concept. For instance, if your concept is the tragedy of communism, the themes you might wish to illustrate will probably include: Lenin as a premature messiah, the failure in general of social engineering, the ironic contrast that particular pieces of social engineering such as the TVA* succeeded under capitalism while their equivalents failed under communism, the Russian dictatorship as a continuation of the reigns of Peter the Great and Ivan the Terrible (there's a good novel on reincarnation in here), and so on. A theme is less than a concept only in the sense that several will fit inside a concept, as can be seen from the fact that any of the themes I have mentioned could conceivably make a concept by itself, with its own subsidiary themes. Themes can be broken down into smaller parts through several layers but that need not bother us because they are treated the same. Developing themes to flesh out a concept is a skill you will have mastered as a new writer and is not specifically addressed in this book.

The concept and its associated themes are abstracts, the large vision of the book. If you are in the middle of other work when they come to you, it is useful to write them down before you lose them or they transmogrify into something less exciting. But the concept should be capable of containment in a single sentence, and all the themes in a large and complicated book, if succinctly stated, would probably fill only a couple of sheets of paper. They are important planning steps whether taken consciously or subconsciously, but the bulk of the planning for a book, whether done all at once and formally on paper or simultaneously with the writing of the book and conducted in your head, normally goes into the next step.

Events   These are the happenings, *the actions of your characters*, that will illustrate your themes (and sub themes) and through them your concept. The non-fiction writer selects his events, and the fiction writer creates his events, to make his

---

* During the Depression the Tennessee Valley Authority built huge dams primarily as a means of providing jobs for dispossessed farmers.

point. This too is something that the novice does instinctively or at least subconsciously, but to which the writer making the transition to professionalism must pay conscious attention to. The process of creating or choosing events is described in books for novices, including the companion volume to this one, *Start Writing Today!*, and there is no need to discuss it here. But this chapter does include much comment on advanced problems with events as they affect other considerations of interest; and the following chapter, A Plotter's Cookbook, is entirely devoted to the optimum *arrangement* of events.

Plot The plot is nothing of itself; it has no existence except as a framework to link the actions of the characters. It is merely a sequence running from a convenient beginning to a more or less logical or emotionally satisfying end. This applies even to the most highly structured genres, like mysteries. Note that every kind of creative writing has a plot, in the sense that a story is told from beginning to end. The 'story' in a philosophical discussion is a marshalling of arguments in a certain order towards a conclusion, and in biography and history the 'story' is a more obviously time-linear progression. The plot is an empty vessel in which the writer arranges his progression of event and character; in practice one arrangement is always so strikingly superior to all other arrangements that the only question for the professional writer is how long he will have to persevere with alternative arrangements before he finds it. There is no mystique to plotting, and treating plotting as an art equal to creating living characters is a disservice I do not intend doing you. Chapter 4 on practical problems with plots should therefore be read like a mechanic's manual.

Character If the plot is a chest in which you carry around events, the event is a drawer in which character is revealed. The characteristics of your characters cause them to behave in a certain way, and this shapes the events in which they are involved, which may in turn alter the character. The line to your reader is through the character, rather than through the concept, theme, plot or event. If the reader does not identify with the character, he will put your book down regardless of the brilliance of your event creation, plot organisation, thematic insight or conceptual universality. If you are one of those very few creative writers, mainly mathematical and linguistic philosophers, who do not write about people and what they do, your characters are your arguments plus as much of your prejudices as are revealed in your writing. Chapter 5 deals specifically with character but in fact all the 'creative' chapters of this book, Chapters 3 to 5 inclusive, are in one way or another about character, because virtually nothing happens without people. Chapter 2 on the ideal reader and Chapter 6 on the writer's personality should also be counted because the writer is always a present character, even if his presence is signalled only by his scrupulous obser- vance of the god's-eye view (in the jargon, the 'third-person impersonal viewpoint'). *Everything* in virtually every branch of creative writing is about character.

The separation of these items is for convenience only. Let us suppose for a moment that Paul Johnson were inclined to accept my classifications – I have no idea whether he would or not – and then add that it is our considered opinion that *A History of the Modern World From 1917 to the 1980s* (also published as *Modern Times*) has as its main concept the damage done to social and political life by the decline in absolute standards of morality. We might also list twenty related themes, extracted from his chapters, which together illustrate this concept. Mr Johnson might however insist that his main concept is that the machinations of the professional politicians with their belief in the power of the intellect to change things for the better is contrary to what we can observe of nature and history. Both points are made with great force in his book but which has primacy (which includes the other) is an arguable matter. The important thing is that all these subdivisions do not matter to the reader because in the end he will take your argument or story as a whole or not at all. And it is through your presentation of character that the reader will accept or reject your concept and themes. Mr Johnson's publishers of record (the ones who first published the book), Weidenfeld and Nicolson, explicitly recognise this on the back of the paperback edition where they refer to his 'ingenious organizational structure, which allows ample space for the vivid incident and the telling anecdote' – vivid incident and telling anecdote are almost by definition about people!

DISCOVERING NEW CONCEPTS

Concept and characters burst upon the novice writer like the light on the road to Damascus. His problems concern attitude and mechanics. The beginning professional will have acquired at least the start of the right attitude and a modest confidence that the mechanical problems he has already solved provide training for those he will still encounter. To balance this, ideas for his next book do not come all that easily or, if he has a notebook in which he enters ideas as they come to him, those he already has often do not seem fabulous enough to inspire the expenditure of the huge amount of time and energy a book consumes. This writer is at a watershed in his career akin to the menopause but, since the watershed typically comes in his twenties, lacks the emotional experience and confidence to handle it that the menopausal person is supposed to have (but in real life frequently does not). He needs a set of guidelines and perhaps tools to help him discover and select a new concept worthy of his talents. The first temptation is to serialise the characters of your first book or books. There are two kinds of serial characters, the natural and the stillborn. I don't know how to distinguish between them except by hindsight.

The stillborn book This occurs when a chief character (or a set of important characters) who has facinated us in his first book is offered up in another book and turns out to be merely tiresome. Though much-used multiple-book characters may eventually become tired even in the hands of a practised professional, they are obviously not stillborn, and it takes many books to reach that stage. The stillborn series character is always dead after a single book, and this normally happens at the beginning of a writer's career except in those cases where it terminates a very brief career, when obviously the failed second book about the character is the cause of the end. Sometimes the stillborn book happens to a practised writer who is a little tired and tries to recycle characters from an earlier book – it happened to me just once – but not all that often.

Essentially the stillborn book comes about because the writer, casting around for the fuel for another book, does not cast far enough or long enough. There may be a shortfall of confidence, a fear of striking out into uncharted waters. One literary agent is convinced the stillborn book is always the result of pure laziness; he absolutely forbids his new writers to use the same characters in two books running and points out that no publisher likes taking serial books from a new writer ('as opposed to their gleeful blackmail of established authors to create serial sets'). Whatever the reason, out comes another book about characters or, worse, situations that have already given their all and have now overstayed their welcome. When I reported remarks by an editor about a writer who kept fruitlessly recycling the joy of the swinging sixties in London, I was deluged with letters from writers who confessed themselves in the same boat (recycling worn-out ideas, not necessarily 'up Carnaby Street without a paddle'); in most cases their second or third books had not been published.

You could try the normal remedies, described elsewhere in this book, but the stillborn book is probably the single unsalvageable disaster likely to strike you; all other bad books can be saved – though whether some should is a different matter.

The solution is not to fall into the trap of the stillborn book in the first place. One occasionally meets a new writer who from the start conceives a trilogy of serious novels, or a continuing character in detective fiction, or a survey of history, that is too ambitious to fit in one volume. His ambition is of course admirable but the advice the hardened professional perforce must give him is to cut back and write one book at a time. This is no reflection on his capacity or will but because the proposer of the series probably has no idea of the scope of the project he so blithely promotes, and will very probably become discouraged and so be lost to the profession and to the entertainment of readers. Underestimating the amount of work involved is a common mistake. A friend of mine, a sophisticated man who has spent the last twenty years of his career around professional writers, closely observing their work methods and foibles, projected a trilogy of novels and spent six months working on the first one – and was surprised and hurt when I told him he had finished little more than a tenth of the actual work and should forget the trilogy, scratch his present manuscript, and instead write one hefty novel*.

One book at a time for the first three books seems good advice, and after that you can start recycling characters if you wish, especially if any of the three books sold well or struck a particular chord with your editor or anyone in the sales department at your publishers. Less frequently the publicity people are also a good sounding board; when Chris Holmes was at Secker & Warburg I profited from paying close attention to his reaction to my books as they appeared.

Serial concepts　It is true that there are some very specialised writers whose range of subjects is sharply circumscribed, but even so in different books they normally attempt to illuminate new concepts, or different aspects of the same concept. Only politicians and fanatics write the same book over and over. But the writers with truly narrow ranges are either academics or supremely expert in their field (I think here of many gardening writers) and already know their next concept. The academic's problem is finding time to write everything he knows. The expert doesn't have a problem because he can always find an aspect of his field he has not covered before and if he cannot think of one his publisher

---

* Anyone reading this who hasn't yet been published should limit their first novel, with the exception of the 'good read' categories like historical fiction, to 100,000 words; the same limit applies to all classes of creative non-fiction. My friend is in the very special position of knowing many writers (some of whom owe him large favours) who can put his manuscript into the hand of a publishing decision-maker as soon as it is ready. An unsolicited overlength manuscript may be, and in many houses will be, rejected by some junior purely on grounds of being too long – without being read by anyone at all.

will be quick to point to a gap in the market. Such writers could be said to be onto natural serial-concepts.

All other non-fiction writers and fiction writers have to search for concepts and must weigh the advantages and disadvantages if what they discover is a serial concept. The most obvious non-fiction series arises when a proposed book is intended to address readers at various stages of development, when it might be better to have a set of two or three or often more books if they are intended for use in formal graded education or self-education. In many markets three inexpensive small books are a better bet than one large expensive one; for other markets the converse is true, and in either case to series or not is *not* the question – you have no choice. You should be receptive to such considerations when put forward by your publisher or, if you are aware of them, mention them to him. This book forms part of a set for three reasons: I am convinced, and the publisher agreed, that the intermediate and established writer will find it irritating to be forced to mine for the information he wants among raw basics for novices; novices don't have the money to pay for thick books of which they can use only part; and most writers do not want a hefty book on their crowded desks when they can instead have one with humbler space requirements.

Various aspects of a subject might each warrant a book; for instance, instruction in advertising copywriting would support at least three separate basic books (on retail, on national branded goods, and on institutional or 'image' advertising, which are the three distinct classes in which advertising is created). But a real expert could easily write three further books of interest to thousands of marketing and advertising executives and writers (on multinational advertising, on the concept of the 'grey' or apparently non-directed but yet functional message, on advanced methods of linking the potential customer to the product through the message). Furthermore there are special considerations in writing advertising for the various media (television, glossy magazines, newspapers, radio, cinema, posters, point of sale, product packaging, direct mail, and so on), each of which might warrant a separate book.

Holes Recently my son bought his first 'big' bicycle and I got a bike too for a spot of bicycle awareness instruction. I was amazed at the number of books on various facets of bicycling on the shelves at my library and at my favorite bookstore, yet a cursory inspection, confirmed by checking *Books in Print*, suggested to me several gaps in the market into which I could fit a bicycling book as soon as I learned to ride my bike and finished the three big novels I have contracted for. Equally, every time I check the computer shelves in libraries and bookstores, I get ten ideas for necessary books that aren't available. These are books that I want, yet no one has written them, and, being mainly a novelist, I never will have the time. Writers who whine about a shortage of ideas just haven't learned to look for the holes.

There's another kind of hole you should look for: the ones on the shelf left by fast-selling books. Even if the readership is well-served, could you offer a publisher a slightly different angle, even a modestly deeper expertise than the writers already on the shelf? The publisher who already has a seller might want an extra string to his bow, but often it is the envious competitor who pays the bigger advance. Look also at those publishers in their own right who distribute books from another, usually foreign but sometimes small local, publisher in a field in which they do not themselves publish: their knowledge of sales in that market may well incline them to dip a toe in the water on their own behalf.

Still another hole. Let's say your area of expertise is French painters, late nineteenth century. Stand before the bookstore shelf (a far more pleasant occupation than studying publishers' catalogues and *Books in Print*, which you will of course also do for confirmation) and consider which publishers in the general field do not have a book in some subject on which your expertise qualifies you to make a proposal. Let's say you're a Gauguin johnny, or would like to make him your speciality, what will you see on the shelf? For sure, Little, Brown has a big Gauguin book, perhaps more than one, and Phaidon and Thames & Hudson ditto. Write their names on your list; they may want another book on Gauguin if your angle is sufficiently different, or even merely in a different price range. If you don't yet have an angle, buy or borrow all the available books and discover what they don't tell you that you want to know. But first see who else publishes art books, and perhaps has a leaning to the late nineteenth-century French, but doesn't have anything available or announced on Gauguin. That's your hole. This publisher might not require an angle at all but merely want a straightforward workmanlike book with which to compete in a market he does not cover. One way to demonstrate your expertise is to tell him in a brief letter what the books already available lack that you will provide (the objection that you don't want to tell him how much competition there is holds no water: if he doesn't already know, he's an incompetent and you want nothing to do with him).

One further hole is the series originated by a publisher to which a number of writers contribute. These desirable spots (quite well-paid, and sales of individual volumes usually benefit from the synergy of promoting a set rather than just one book) are mostly reserved for established writers or leading experts who are invited by the publishers to contribute. Very often, however, editors can become desperate to find someone for the more obscure bits so that it does no harm to write in along the lines, 'Your series of books on ABC is incomplete without a discussion of XYZ. If you don't already have someone lined up...'

Serial characters For fiction writers possession of a serial character or set of serial characters may be a mixed blessing. Arthur Conan Doyle was convinced Holmes and Watson kept him from the serious literary and medical fame he deserved – an incredibly common delusion among the creators of vastly popular art but especially in the fields of literature and music; one wonders what Arthur Conan Doyle would say were he alive to discover that, though the names of the men whose 'serious' reputations he so envied are now forgotten, his work alone survives the test of time, the only objective test of literature. Conan Doyle lived into the first generation of critics who snobbishly excluded from the pantheon of literature anything that sold well because it could be appreciated by a large number of readers – how he would have appreciated John Braine's Yorkshire-blunt remark that 'All classics are best sellers,' and Fay Weldon's snide but true quip that '"literature" [is the] invention of twentieth-century critics'! Just to keep the record straight, Mr Braine promptly added that not all bestsellers are classics.

Serial characters are about serious money. From a publisher's viewpoint, they have nothing to do with giving the author an easy ride and everything to do with giving the sales force the easiest possible victory in the battle with the other publishers' representatives for the retailers' limited shelf space. Best of all is a series from a proven bestselling author, then a singleton from a proven bestseller, then a series from a middle-ranking steady-selling writer, then a singleton from the middleranker. Low sellers and new writers divide what's left, though often quality books and deserving newcomers are favoured with a special reserve of space in good bookstores – indeed, the best bookstores are most easily identified by stock reaching well beyond bestsellers. The series from an established author is also an easy choice for the bookseller, and readers who were sorry when the characters left them at the end of the last book in the series can once more find solace in the near-familiar.

A publisher may not welcome a series from a new writer, because he knows the chances are it will be bad, for the reasons described above, but he is always keen for a series from a proven writer. It is instructive to follow the steps by which a writer becomes the creator of a series, even if it is perforce a haphazard process and unique in each case. Among Andrew McCoy's published novels only one shares no characters with any of the others. Did he plan it that way when he started writing? 'Not at all. I had finished one book, *Atrocity Week*, which I felt had to be written, which was fiction only because the true story I wanted to tell would have fallen foul of the libel laws. I wanted to write another, but somewhat more fictional. *The Insurrectionist* was about revolution in South Africa. It happened that two of the characters with walk-on parts in *Atrocity Week* were, respectively, a professional revolutionary with reason to hate the

South Africans, and the second-in-command of BOSS, the South African Bureau of State Security. I took them as the main characters for *The Insurrectionist* and gave each about half the book. This too was a book with a message, that violence does not pay. By this time the writing bug had got me and I wanted to write a more straightforward adventure, pure entertainment. *Atrocity Week* had been published and become a bestseller and my hardcover publishers, Secker & Warburg in London, had good reports on *The Insurrectionist*, still unpublished, and had sold it for paperback on the day they contracted for it, so they commissioned *African Revenge* from me, a novel of adventure based rather loosely on my experience hunting crocodiles in the Congo. In this book I needed a deus ex machina, an off-stage warning voice with punch, so once more I wheeled out Burger [the BOSS 2-I-C] and his paramilitary Special Security Police for a couple of small appearances.' Thus, after three books, you didn't have a series in the accepted sense but were evolving towards it? 'It was accidental. I came to a breakpoint in a novel, needed a character, and used one I already had because he hit the spot. Creating credible characters is so difficult, one doesn't waste a good one thoughtlessly, or lightly create a new one from scratch.' Was there editorial pressure to recycle these characters? 'There were comments that such-and-such was an appealing character, and almost an orchestration of remarks that killing off the engaging revolutionary, Iningwe, was not smart – but at the time, being pretty inexperienced, I saw no reason to attach special importance to these remarks. However, there was pressure to stick for my next book to the general area of Africa, where all my three books up to that time had been set. After *The Insurrectionist* was reviewed on the main BBC *News* by the Director of the Institute for Strategic Studies, and the novelist John Braine praised *African Revenge* in *The Sunday Telegraph*, the pressure became obvious and open. Secker's editorial director John Blackwell even offered a concept to build the story around: the last elephants killed for their ivory. Meanwhile I had lunch with my paperback publisher, Nick Austin, who was interested in the ex-Nazis I had met while playing polo in

South America, and he offered to commission an adventure set in South America as an original paperback to keep him going while I sorted out the elephant book. This paperback original was *Cain's Courage*. At one point in it I wanted one of the characters, a pilot named Tanner Chapman, to refer to someone really tough and for this purpose imagined the hero of *African Revenge*, Lance Weber, a few years on from that adventure. Suddenly all my troubles with the elephant book, which Nick Austin suggested we call *Blood Ivory*, fell away. I had an idea, from John Blackwell, a title from Nick, the setting of Africa because there was no choice, a hero in Lance Weber, even a secondary character in this pilot who would have to be written in to account for his remark in *Cain's Courage*. Once you have your main character, devising a story is a cinch. In fact an idea for a third Lance Weber story sprung from this conjunction of existing characters.' So even at this stage the series was developing more or less unplanned? 'Yes. I did another paperback original for Nick, *The Meyersco Helix*, which somehow turned out to be my only book that has no characters in common with any of the other books, and after that I was casting around for an idea and Nick asked what happened to Lance Weber, adding that he would be happy to buy the subsidiary rights in another Lance Weber adventure. Secker then commissioned *Lance of God*, the third of the Lance Weber books.' Could such a series be planned from scratch? 'It must be possible, in the sense that nothing is impossible. But the series that arises by happenstance and reaction to circumstance is the stronger for the random branches it possesses, not when seen from the aspect of the individual books but viewed as a complete, continuing story. Series that are too much planned always read as if they were strained through too fine a muslin – no vitamins.' But, besides being set in Africa, surely *some* consciously planned facets link these Lance Weber books? 'His skill as a long-distance traveller under adverse and perhaps hostile conditions is a basic building block in each book. However, this was not planned but inherited from the first book, in which his brother put him in control of the convoy to keep him busy.'

Recognising serial concepts and characters is no different from recognising singleton ideas but can be made more difficult because so often you find them in your own work or field of intense expertise where, paradoxically, your proximity to the subject can blind you to even the most appealing of possibilities. Be on your guard.

Recognising concepts   For all novices, and for most levels of professional writers who are not too unlucky, concept recognition is tautological: it is the right concept for you if it strikes you as the right concept for you. Most of us read so widely in the writings of our peers and in the background material we use for our books that a constant stream of concepts and variants offer themselves. But we all have flat spots and unlucky days, and it is on these that we choose the wrong concept and start the long, frustrating process of writing a bad book. The professional writer must first guard against choosing a concept that is not suitable for him. The same tools and tests that protect against selecting the wrong concept will inevitably select the right concept.

The first essential is to be organised. Those balmy days of your first and perhaps second book when you knew what you wanted to write about, knew that was the only book to write, knew precisely what you wished to say, are gone. You cannot expect to sit down at your desk and immediately have a new concept pop out of the air – your original concept or concepts did not arise like that either, though it may have seemed like it at the time. You should have a file in which you keep concepts that strike you. A single sentence or even a phrase will do, or a cutting from a newspaper or magazine; personally I prefer the shortest possible phrase on a single sheet of paper, so that I can sort the sheets into related stacks if I'm stuck for a concept. Some other writers, of both fiction and non-fiction, have large filing systems in which they keep extensive cuttings and cross-referenced notes but these are, I suspect, to a large extent make-work to protect the writer from actually writing. In this respect as in others the author travels furthest who travels leanest. There may be exceptions to this rule but they are few. For example, even a writer so dependent on the facts in his files as the espionage historian Richard Deacon creates books that almost inevitably become standard reference sources more by an excellent memory and an incisive intelligence (to draw inferences from disparate and incomplete facts) than from any structure that even the cleverest filing system can impose. In any event, you must know your concept before you can start building up a file of subsidiary information; the paralysis that will result from the 'total information store' the silicon gurus dream of is as fine a definition of madness as the Tower of Babel. Eventually this file (or filing cabinet) will hold more ideas than you can ever use; don't throw the old ones out, they will gradually move to the back and eventually become totally meaningless. You need spend no time organising, sorting and maintaining this file of ideas; when you have a new idea spend a minute making a note on a sheet of paper, pop it in the file, close the file and put it away. If you think of or come across a subsidiary point, make a quick note on the same sheet as the concept or pop the cutting into the same file. Don't be tempted to waste time speculating about the whole superstructure of a new book rather than writing the difficult bits of the book you presently have under construction.

The time to assess the contents of your ideas file is when you are coming up to the start of a new book. Three to six months before you want to start the book should be enough time. Sort through your ideas – after a few years you will sort only through the top inch or so of stuff – until you have a few possible concepts, two or three or up to a double handful. Don't choose too many – watch out for information overload! You will notice that some of your phrases have become quite meaningless: far from inspiring a concept for a whole book, they do not even suggest a complete sentence. The distance of time has proven their unworthiness and you need not grieve for their loss; they would, if pursued, have caused you untold pain and frustration. Others, while clear, merely leave you cold. As an example, I have an idea for a novel on plastic surgery which has over about twelve years built up a file of its own quite three inches thick, more material than I could possibly use. Despite the fact that a publisher is interested, every time I open this file I fail to recover that first enthusiasm which caused me to note the concept and discuss it with publishers – it is very probably, in my hands at least, a dead concept. Spend a whole day making your selection of the possibles and by all means daydream about their possibilities, as long as you do your dreaming with a pencil in hand, making notes.

Now try to put the possibles out of your mind. Go back to what you were doing (if you have a proper rhythm and cycle of books in writing, lying fallow, and rewriting, you are probably busy on a polishing job) and finish that. It will be impossible to put the new concepts right out of your mind and gradually, over a good deal of time, the best one will announce itself, so that when you are ready to start work on the book, the actual choice will not be at all hard, and you will have noted down many of the thematic points necessary to build the concept. Note that again we let Father Time and the subconscious make a choice. If this sort of talk reminds you uncomfortably of Third-Eye jiggery-pokery, consider it instead as the equivalent of psyching yourself up to jog in all weathers while keeping in mind your doctor's advice that your body knows its own rhythms best and that when you reach the threshold of real pain, you should stop. Your subconscious watches out for your best interests in exactly the same way. Elsewhere I have written of the stupid envy my 'accursed fecundity' inspires in writers who are blessed with far better natural imaginations than mine; their problem is that they won't make the very small effort necessary to put their imaginations in gear, and typically they won't believe my explanation that my felicity with new concepts is acquired by simple exercises conducted persistently over a period of years. There are also writers who do not follow this scheme – the file with concepts written down, selection, time for subconscious winnowing and acceptance – who have no problem sitting down and starting a new book, but they are typically high-level novelists who produce no more than a book every two or three years and who write about aspects of the same concept over and over again; their file is so thin that they can carry it in their heads at all times, more often than not because it is their own lives they are regurgitating!

The problem with this whole process of discovering which of the competing concepts you really want is that it takes an inordinate amount of time. This time is not wasted because, by the subconscious nature of the activity, you are not only permitted but encouraged to do something productive at the same time. There are many writers who have several apparently idle months between finishing one book and starting the next; they sit in front of their typewriter staring vacantly, they change the music on the player but cannot tell you what is playing, or they take long walks. ('I know when he's starting a new book,' a shopkeeper says of a famous thriller-writer who lives down the coast. 'He comes in here and can't remember what he came to buy.') They either believe consciously that one should compartmentalise books by finishing one before you start another, or have never discovered that it is possible to save several months by allowing an overlap. If you have already finished your last book when you read this and you have an absolutely blank mind about your next book, you could scour the papers and the newscasts for a story but it would be far better for you to resign yourself to spending three months in relative idleness while you build up a small file of concepts. Set a time, say three months hence, to make a shortlist, and another time, a month or six weeks later, to start writing; meanwhile spend most of your time reading and thinking but do something else as well (develop an interest in a subject and write a saleable article about it) so that your subconscious can be opened up for bonuses. Having learned the lesson, every time something strikes you in future make a note and pop it into the file and you will never again have to waste time.

But that's not my sort of thing An exhaustive list of the sources of concepts is neither possible nor desirable because it would by implication exclude other possible sources. What is important is that you must not close your mind to any possible source of concepts, or the supplementary material that makes concepts usable. When it was suggested to me through my agent that I write a novel on the concept of blowing a skyscraper down floor by floor to rescue the hostages held by terrorists on the top floor, the idea did not instantly illuminate a globe over my head (too technical; too much suspension of disbelief required; hostage-type books likely to become too common; tricky but without any depth of novelty). But I cautiously begged permission to keep it for a few months to see if it would grow on me before it was offered to another writer. Hardly six weeks later I was idly leafing through one of my wife's books on geological formations when the news of a big sinkhole in Florida came on the television. Bingo! In my novel *Sinkhole* the building that had to be blown down was placed in the bottom of the sinkhole on an unstable island floating in a sea of flammable oil – right in the spot required to land the rescue helicopter. It all came to me in that instant. Normally geological formations bore me stiff and I would certainly not buy or borrow a book on them, and I don't watch the television news regularly because it is offensively shallow (instead I listen to current affairs programmes on the BBC World Service); the point is that I didn't reject these inputs simply because they came from sources I do not view with enthusiasm. It is for this reason that you should leave ideas that have lost their shine in the back of your file: you never know when additional knowledge will suddenly revive them. Returning to *Sinkhole* for a moment, I already knew about sinkholes and had even seen some years before, so something else could have triggered the association and the resulting book, though it might have taken years (which in this case were not available because the original idea was not my own – but the time available for your own concepts to mature is unlimited). In particular, you should guard against bricking yourself off from information merely because it isn't from a 'literary' source. The primary source of your material is irrelevant: it is what you do with the material that creates literature or otherwise.

Specialist research   There is no separate chapter on research in this book because the aspirant professional who has survived his novitiate already knows more than enough about research: he knows to avoid wasting time on speculative research, on principle to spend on research only the time necessary to do the job competently, and to do as much research as possible after writing the first draft so that every minute spent on research is purpose-directed. Note that the general reading you do for pleasure in your allocated leisure time, even if intimately related to the book you are currently writing, does not count as 'research'; what we are concerned with here is time wasted reading reams of material in the hope of finding something useful, which more often than not is only an excuse for not working.

There is one type of research that the beginning professional is probably not familiar with, unless he is by profession an academic or certain class of specialised journalist. This is specialist research conducted for you by someone else, perhaps a professional researcher, because you lack either the expertise or the time to do the job. The most common kind of researcher can be found on your television screen where they are credited in non-fiction and sometimes faction programmes; the next most common specialist researcher-for-hire is probably the picture researcher, who finds photographs to illustrate books, but there are specialist researchers available in virtually every subject under the sun though finding the more obscure ones may be a job for another specialist. You can find some of the more general researchers listed in writers' annuals, for instance in *Writers' & Artists' Yearbook* in the section *Editorial, Literary and Production Services*. Institutions of tertiary education, galleries and museums have people who, if they are not knowledgeable in a field themselves, keep experts on call who may be willing to do your research for a fee. Or you can write through his publisher to the expert who wrote the standard text, if there is one, but generally he will be too busy on his own next book to do research for you, and will probably charge more too.

Before engaging an expert, you should first ascertain a) that you really cannot do the job yourself and b) that you are willing to bear the risks involved in stamping your imprimatur on 'facts' discovered by someone else.

You may know absolutely nothing about chemistry but require a poison in your story. Fine. You don't need a specialist researcher. Invent a poison! When you have finished the book, a local doctor or chemist will be only too happy, if approached in the right way, to read the relevant sections and tell you what poison would suit the circumstances you invented and what changes you should make for increased credibility. Or go to the nearest university library and hire a medical or chemistry student for the price of a meal for a couple of hours to help you through the medical abstracts. That's probably what most professional researchers will do, except that they will bill you for their time as well as the price of two meals. One researcher told me that half the time she performs to the eminent satisfaction of her clients without doing anything more strenuous than photocopying from the books given as source references in the *Encyclopaedia Britannica*; do you wonder that she considers most authors have more money than brains? Another researcher has a big microcomputer installed in his office to impress clients but in fact writes away to databases for printouts to be sent by post; logging on and searching the databases would be too expensive even if he knew how to use the computer, which he doesn't, but all the same he charges 'connect-time' by the hour! I want to stress that both these researchers give value for money – their resentment and contempt arises because they feel underused; like all good researchers, they burn to be stretched to the limit.

Incompetent researchers have their own solidarity and of course their victims don't like to admit they made fools of themselves. But I was amazed to discover that one very competent best-selling author had written a Regency novel (historical, not romance) without even discovering the name of Captain Gronow, the most perceptive and amusing social diarist of the period. His researcher, unless utterly incompetent, *must* have come across the good captain. But because the writer saw only the information digests which did not mention Gronow's name, he missed the chance to include another very real character with a lot of pithy ready-made dialogue. This writer still farms out his research, but now hires three researchers to do the same job. Since many of his novels are heavily laden with verifiable facts, he must be spending BMW money for a job he could do better and more quickly himself.

For all these reasons I prefer doing my own research whatever the cost in time and travel. When I move outside my own knowledge and require expert (rather than student) guidance I prefer to find someone I can speak to face-to-face or at least on the phone; in my view an accessible expert in person is always superior to the leading expert strained through a third-party filter. One advantage is that I have yet to receive a bill, though for my novel *Iditarod* just the international phone bills of experts on wolves and human endurance and hypothermia returning my calls must have come to thousands of dollars. A friend who deliberately ignores international politics wanted to write a book in which chemical warfare substances play a part, and couldn't make head or tail of the implications of the set of *Time Magazine* clippings he had gathered. He called Imperial College, London, because the author of the best book in his library was a professor there; my friend asked the secretary if there was a graduate student he could approach, for a fee of course, for a one- or two-page appreciation, and was put through to the professor himself, who in three minutes told him precisely what he wanted to know. The writer says, 'It wasn't just spot-on information, it was so right I used the prof's exact words as dialogue for the President.' Significantly, even legal experts in practice, as distinct from academe, have never charged me for advice to be used in a novel rather than for, say, contesting income tax claims or libel suits.*

A good researcher tells you instantly if he can't or won't do the job, agrees a fixed price for the job beforehand, quotes an hourly rate for supplementary work done at your specific request, demands specific and clear instructions as to the scope of the information required, has no hesitation in telling

---

* Lawyers are always being badmouthed for avarice but when I was fighting the arbitrary suppression of one of my books by a supposedly liberal publisher, several top legal minds offered time and advice free of charge either to me direct or to the civil liberties organisations who had interested themselves in my problem.

you his sources, and will often recommend someone else for either the whole job or very specialised parts of it. The value of a good researcher is not so much in the facts he can find out for you (there are *no* facts he can find that you cannot discover for yourself) but that he may possess the experience, training or contacts which enable him to analyse and interpret the information in a way that you are not equipped to do. Such paragons are hard to find and expensive but well worth it.

Transforming the everyday   A London publisher tells a lovely story about approaching the éminence grise behind an important politician to write his memoirs, which were expected to recount the covering up of several scandals involving people still in the public eye, even the odd assassination, plus some Anglo-American dirty washing. 'Whoever would be interested,' exclaimed the éminence, much surprised, 'in what we did every day? No, no, no! It would be utterly boring.' Sang-froid doesn't get any more British than that. Nor more narrowly parochial. You may not rub up against the great and the good (publishers would for purely commercial reasons prefer them to be great and bad) every day but you do meet people and there could well be concepts in these people. Compassion and altruism are universal qualities, as are greed and lust. Your book will in any event be constructed from the actions of your characters and it is useful to remind yourself occasionally that the qualities of the rich and the powerful are the same as those of the poor and the powerless: they behave the same in all but degree – and their behaviour is the same because their primary motivations of survival and propagation do not differ. Since you learn about character from those around you (as well as from books and television and films and newspapers), you might easily be able to distill a concept from the semi-conscious observations of your fellows which you make all your waking hours. For instance, the idea in my files for a novel on plastic surgery was suggested to me by the behaviour of a friend who, after corrective surgery following a car crash, had several sessions of elective cosmetic surgery which seemed to me to be driven by a spiral of self-destructive vanity. Another instance: any listener to the BBC Radio 4 arts

magazine *Kaleidoscope* over a period of years will know that
it is a cliché for mystery writers to say that they find their plots
in the peculiarities of their neighbours' characters and
behaviour. The best mystery writers make everything except
the murder seem very ordinary and the rest try to emulate
them, which may account for their awareness of their sources.
Whatever your line of writing, you can do worse than to copy
this awareness of the real people around you. At the very least,
your fictional or non-fictional characterisation will be
improved by first-hand observation of living characters.

Adapting a concept from elsewhere   Good writing has
several kinds of subtexts, some intended by the writer and
others unintended, though some of the latter might be recog-
nisable only to other writers. It is among these throwaway
lines of other writers that many of us find goldmines. These
lines or paragraphs or implications seem, at least to the taker,
either to be misused by the writer in whose work we find
them or not given the prominence their excitement seems to
demand (though of course the first writer will defend himself
on grounds of balance and truth). As an example, my novel
The Zaharoff Commission was inspired by an incident
described in less than two pages in Donald McCormick's
excellent standard biography of Zaharoff, *Pedlar of Death*;
of course I was fascinated by the character exposed in the rest
of a thoroughly researched biography, and of course Mr
McCormick, a scrupulous journalist and historian rather
than a novelist, was limited in what he could say by what was
known or what could reasonably be deduced from the deter-
minable facts. But what attracted me was the very mystery of
the events which caused the premier of France to say that
Zaharoff had shortened the war by a year. Mr McCormick
spent a quarter-century unearthing the layers of obfuscation
Zaharoff delighted in drawing over himself, yet told me that
he did not feel he had fully fathomed the man's character; he
generously added that my novelistic extensions had further
illuminated Zaharoff for him. Much was made by knowledgeable critics about the historical accuracy of the novel,
but the concept came to me with such force precisely because

there is, for practical reasons, never likely to be a more complete biography than Mr McCormick's of one of the key but least-known shapers of our century.

'*A clever animal, knowing it is being pursued, can always lead its hunters to disaster.*' This line is actually in quotes and in italics in Brian Freemantle's thriller, *Charlie Muffin's Uncle Sam*, where Charlie, deep in trouble, remembers being told this by his late mentor. As it might be taken as a key to all the Charlie Muffin books, it is an easy choice but a good one: surely no reader of this book is so dull that he cannot think of a dozen stories arising from that concept? There is no point in insulting your intelligence with further examples from fiction. If reading the work of another writer whom you admire does not suggest plenty of ideas to you, why are you reading him? Chekhov suggests nothing to me except boredom, but I cannot read Dostoyevsky without getting at least one idea for a book of mine per page of his. Since Dostoyevsky is the greatest prose writer who ever lived such a reaction is not surprising but every other good writer manages to generate the same phenomenon if to a lesser degree. A favourite of mine is Richard Condon not only for his scrupulous regard for words and his talent for the amusingly bizarre, but because he always offers other writers plenty to pilfer. Of course the general reader and the professional writer have in common that they read an author because he rings a bell with them – anything from shared prejudices to noble aspirations – but the professional writer when he reads is, in addition to being stroked, educating and perhaps enriching himself.

The permissible limits of using other people's work   There need be no embarrassment about where your ideas come from. On the single occasion that another writer told me the concept for his novel was inspired by a line in one of my books, I a) was surprised that he should be so tactless as to refer to a book I should like to rewrite totally, b) couldn't remember the line, c) didn't think when told where to find the line that it was such hot stuff, and d) saw only the most tenuous connection between my point and his novel, certainly nothing like the possibility of plagiarism which bothered him. The reason for the difference in importance we attach to the line is that to him it is a concept, to me it is something necessary to put down in a hurry so that my reader and I can get on with important business; the concept selected the writer, as we have seen already. It isn't my sort of concept at all but for the purpose of this book I spent an hour trying to imagine what I would have done with the idea and couldn't come up with anything from the same seed that would remotely resemble his story. It is possible writers underestimate the generosity of other writers. Like my friend just described, I was worried when I finished *The Zaharoff Commission* about the possibility of unpleasantness because I had spent several years on independent research without uncovering anything significant that was not already in Donald McCormick's standard biography of Zaharoff and my book was therefore almost entirely sourced from his book (there were other books available but they were little short of ideologically-inspired condemnatory tracts and consequently useless to me). Mr McCormick not only generously reassured me that I had not failed as a researcher because at that late stage it was probably impossible to discover anything more of significance, but read my book in manuscript and gave me a plug that my publishers used on the dust-jacket. Short of outright plagiarism – taking another writer's characters and story directly, which is of course theft and should be discouraged and punished – there is no reason you should not take concepts that other writers, so to speak, throw out with the bathwater. Nor should you be embarrassed about taking another writer's methods and techniques for your own use because that is how such things come into general use and can be tested against the largest possible number of readers to see if they are worth keeping.

WARNING SHOTS

We have now reached the end of the positive side of concept selection, which can be summarised as lying back and enjoying it happening to you, or how to get large rewards for keeping a thin file and doing plenty of what you love best, reading. Unfortunately, for the professional author there are some negative aspects of concept selection. As a professional, you already know about problems with government censorship and that there are certain subjects that are untouchable if you wish to keep on living (Islam) or too difficult to get published (pederasty, though its turn will come, as sodomy's did) and so on. These are in a sense environmental problems of your trade about which you can make your own moral judgements; the professional author who makes his living at his typewriter does not spend much time on these structural taboos. But there are some other constraints you may not be aware of, which we can divide into problems peculiar to publishing and problems particular to individual publishers.

Of the latter little can be said for fear of the libel laws but you can take it that virtually all book publishers, slow payers included, do in fact pay writers all the royalties due. Far more important and frustrating for the professional writer is the key individual at your publishing house who resists making a decision on your work until you are on the verge of going elsewhere, and the firms and individuals prone to political infighting who use your work as sacrificial shock troops so that your book is accepted/rejected/promoted beyond its merits (for which the chickens will come home to roost when you want to sell the company another book) without you knowing why all this is happening. There is no good advice I can give you about this, for the simple reason that the author is always the last to find out, and most never do find out because they lack the sneaky skills required for low-level industrial espionage. Two aspects of the more general, publishing-wide peculiarities merit our consideration:

A tight focus on your work   There are publishers too sophisticated or proud to take the easy choice of serial characters – we're not even discussing the schlock merchants at the pop-biog and gimmick end of the market – but even these want what the cultured New York agent David Stewart Hull deplores as 'more of the same'. It is a phenomenon we have already met in its guise as a perfectly valid commercial impulse. At the top end of the publishing spectrum you will hear it described as 'a tight focus on your work'. Publishers may not tell you outright that they have a bundle invested in creating a readership for you and that the readers don't want novelty, they want the same 'good stuff' they have come to expect from you, but you may take the publishers' motive as read. Publishers hate their good writers to be 'all over the place' in their concepts because that interferes with marketing to the predefined 'segments'.

A 'tight focus on your work' need not necessarily be a gag on creativity but whether it becomes a drag on your output or the stepping stones of your rise and rise is more a matter of your attitude than the facts of the case. If you are convinced the publisher has your best interests at heart, you might bend a little. If you sincerely believe he has in mind only his quarterly report to the stockholders, you should go elsewhere. The best publishers guide you very gently indeed but there is no doubt that they do try to influence their authors – this is one of the reasons many important authors refuse to accept commissions, preferring to write books they really want to write 'on spec' and then delivering them 'take it or leave it' plus or minus such 'editorial input' as will leave the original theme unscathed. My own attitude is that a writer is part of a team and the other guys on the team are top specialists who can be assumed to be on-side until proven otherwise. The editors and publishers who commission books from me will go down the drain right behind me if they advise me wrongly, so I always listen carefully to what experienced people say, and give brownie points for the number of years they have published my books. If I know a book is impossible for me, I always refuse it. A book you start with a resentful frame of mind is already a disaster. On the other hand, don't let unrealistic ambition cause you to reject sound advice: one would normally expect journalists to be rationally objective people, but a publisher tells of one who turned down an offer to write a biography of a pop star with the words, 'What do you think I am, a hack? I'm going to write a novel that'll win the Booker.'* An author with a

* This is the Booker Prize, given annually to a novel in English first published in the

sense of survival, offered a book he doesn't want (as distinct from one he knows he cannot do), tries for a two-book deal of the book the publisher wants plus the one he really wants to do. You need publishers quite as much as they need you.

A tight focus on your work does not mean serial characters but merely that the publisher would like you to stick to one well-defined area. If you write espionage thrillers, you'll earn no bonuses for insisting on writing a romance. A non-fiction writer who suddenly insists he wants to be a novelist is likely to be regarded with some suspicion, because many publishers consider these to be separate trades and their received wisdom is that the author who can handle both successfully is a rare animal. It works the other way as well. When I announced my intention of writing a non-fiction book, one of my publishers went as far as to point out that an established novelist on his list enjoys a certain prestige which could only be tarnished by writing non-fiction.

If you're with a sensible publisher and you don't get your back up the moment he mentions his own more commercial problems, a compromise can usually be reached which will give him his tight focus, seen from the marketing end, and allow you to write what you want without compromising the integrity of your concepts – and we're still talking of the same book. For instance, if you wish to move on from murder mysteries to writing about politics and the human condition, there need be no conflict between a publisher and his author,

UK during that year. Novels are entered for the prize by their publishers. Their authors must be citizens of the Commonwealth or of certain other countries that were formerly part of the British Empire. It's like the Pulitzer and a Guggenheim Fellowship all rolled up, only better because there's only one per year, so that no one else can have one. Unfortunately, the prize is in disrepute because of the judges' tendency to bypass the meritorious for the politically fashionable. However, Booker judges change every year and there have been some quite recent decisions of great merit, like giving the prize to Thomas Keneally. The other top British prize, of better repute if not without recent blemish, is the Whitbread, normally given for straight literary merit rather than extraneous reasons. To declare my interests, a pseudonymous novel of mine was entered by my publishers for the Booker in 1979 and I was once a management consultant to Whitbread, the brewery, not the prize itself. The £50,000 Guinness Peat Aviation prize, given in Ireland where many writers live tax-free, is probably the biggest financial bonanza in literature short of getting the Nobel, but it too is tarnished through attempts at trendiness; recently the prize had to be given twice in the same year because the judges wanted to give it to a book by a powerful critic while their literary consultant, no less an expert than the great Graham Greene, wanted the prize given to a novel of real merit by a less ostentatiously promoted and connected writer.

given only mutual respect. You simply write your murder mystery against a background of such politics as will illustrate the points you intend making about the human condition. To make any contrary argument stick, you must produce a publisher who would not be happy to receive a book like Scott Turow's *Presumed Innocent*, which in its first year sold over 700,000 hardcover copies. Just to hammer the point home, another murder mystery which enjoyed high critical success and became a megaseller was Umberto Eco's *The Name of the Rose*, which could also be described as a religious novel or an historical novel.

One veteran agent insists that when an author and publisher cannot agree on a subject and its treatment the cause is hardly ever literary, but should be sought in some hidden resentment about other matters that neither wants to mention – usually because they are too petty – or in the pretensions of new writers who will never become professionals. In short, he does not recognise the possibility of any valid reason for not compromising, on the part of the writer with the publisher's wish for a 'tight focus', and on the part of the publisher with the writer's desire to stretch his creative inventiveness.

The received wisdom of the trade   These are the no-noes of publishers and film, television and stage producers you must take into account in your selection of concepts. They change over time: we all know that once upon a time lesbianism was acceptable on stage but not in films, and that within the memory of writers still working it was unacceptable to take the mickey out of the clergy or the medical profession on the BBC, neither of which taboo now remains. Some of the current no-noes are illustrated in the next section but no list can ever be complete and the best possible advice is to ignore them: if you really want to write screenplays for 'ice'-movies, a longtime Hollywood no-no, it might be harder to find a producer who bucks the mainstream but sooner or later you will find him. Much more important are the prejudices of your existing publisher, or a producer you already work with or expect to work with regularly.

Studying the market   As an aspirant-writer, you were no doubt advised ad nauseam to study the market. No one but a fool would advise you not to study the environment in which you operate. But the imponderables that you could never hope to discover by reading the trade press far outweigh what you can find out. The inside information is locked up in your publisher's mind. Here is a telephone conversation I had with a publisher who has either published my books in paperback reprint or originated (commissioned) them ever since I started. He is now at the fourth publishing house at which he has, in the apt New York jargon, sponsored my work. It is safe to assume that, insofar as is compatible with his employer's profit and loss sheet, he is on my side; he is that very desirable editor, an enthusiast before he is a publisher. Six weeks before the conversation here reported I had sent him twenty proposals for novels, most of them no more than a paragraph or two on a single sheet of paper. After the amenities, I say,

'Did you read the outlines I sent you?' This is not an idle question. He publishes something approaching a thousand books every year and his time is tightly scheduled.

'I glanced at them. Let me get the file.' A short pause while paper rustles on the line. 'Listen, these horror stories won't do.'

'You asked for those outlines. About three years ago. At the time I had other commitments.'

'Maybe three years ago... One of our sister companies now publishes C— B—. The market won't take straightforward occult stories any more. If you're really enthusiastic about – '

'No, they were never more than a sideshow. Bin them. What about the serious political thing, about Eisenhower and Harry Luce and Senator Taft?'

Rustle of paper. 'I know you do heavy politics well and, personally, I like it, but as a *British* publisher... you'd have a better chance selling it in the States.' More rustle of paper while he presumably speed-reads the proposals grouped with it.

Meanwhile, on the assumption that honesty is always the best policy, and sooner or later he will find out anyway because all these big publishers talk to each other, I tell him, 'In New York St Martin's hated it and David [Hull, my NY literary agent] isn't keen either.'

'And the problem with it is, there's no tight focus on your work here. What do you do after that? None of these other [political] proposals are really related. The good one is historical faction and the others are straight fiction.'

'Okay, you want a tight focus, turn to the proposal for *The Thrill of it All*: it's a single sheet with a bar graph psychoprofile at the top.' This story is about motor racing, but he already knows I was once a motor racer, so I say, 'I spent a year in South America playing polo, and I raced from Cape Town to Rio in a sixty-eight-foot yacht of my own design. That's three novels with a tight focus on glamorous sports. After that, I'll think of something. Maybe you would like to buy me a hot-air balloon.'

'And no doubt they will be hard-hitting books. The truth is, André, there isn't a public there at all, except for Dick Francis. Sports novels that don't bomb, except his, are exceptions to the rule.'

'Listen, pal, did you actually read *Iditarod* before you bought it?' This is a novel I took away from another publisher who had commissioned it but then jerked me around for six years. I lost patience, told them they were in breach of contract and could whistle for the return of their advance, and promptly sold the book to the publisher I am now talking to, who had then told me his house would like to be my publishers of record (jargon for 'main publisher').

'I read enough to know it's good stuff. I also had enthusiastic reports.'

'Yes, but did they tell you the story is about a dog-sled race, a sporting event set in Alaska?'

'I know all that. But the book will sell well in Canada. Regional interest adds the necessary edge.' While this conversation has been progressing, there has been rustling as he glances at the various sheets of my proposals. 'I know *The Zaharoff Commission* did well for you, but I'm still wary of books that are set in a period too far away to be nostalgic but not far enough to be historic.'

That accounts for another handful of my proposals. 'Shit! I'd better send you some more ideas.'

'What about this *Dzerzhinsky Square* proposal? Your forte in the books under your own name, as I see it, is the quality novel with distinct elements of suspense.'

'*Dzerzhinsky Square* was thrown in to make up the round number. It's recycled from that ten-book *Power* proposal you thought too ambitious eight or nine years ago. I'm keen on the idea, or I would not show it again, but it would need two hundred thousand words to do the concept justice.'

'I like it. Don't worry about the length, concentrate on the quality. We can put a higher cover price on a thicker book. Will you promise me a couple of companion volumes so that this isn't a singleton?'

'Of course. Say one about the CIA and another about British Intelligence?'

'All right. Send me something on paper that I can discuss with our sales people, and I'll come back to you with an offer. Nice doing business with you, as usual. Cheerio.'

The surprising thing about this conversation isn't that I ended up with a three-book commission, or even that I nearly didn't – I would have ended up with some kind of deal because the decision to publish my books had already been made and sooner or later I would have hit on an idea that my publisher felt he could sell, or he would have come up with a suggestion acceptable to me. No, the point is the Kafkaesque tone of the whole conversation, the number of things even a professional author doesn't know, and probably cannot be expected to know, about the business that puts the bread on his table.

Three of many examples of ignorance on my part exposed by this conversation are immediately relevant to aspirant professionals. It could be argued that I should have discovered up front that the publisher of Mr C— B— is a sister company, and that, from long association with this particular publisher (the person, not the house) I should have known or guessed that he is likely to protect a leading writer in a field from competition on his own list because that makes commercial sense (for reasons too technical to go into here but ultimately related to the shelf space available in bookstores and the manner in which the dominant wholesale and retail chains buy titles). But such knowledge would not have saved me from wasting three or four days on my three now-unusable horror outlines and would certainly not help the aspirant professional, who is far better served by the assumption that a house which publishes any genre is keenly on the lookout for more authors/books in that genre.

The second example is even more basic: length. When I started writing, I was told by James Oliver Brown, the doyen of American agents, that length limits should be taken as upper absolutes. That is still true for the beginner, though the goalposts have moved. As I write, 70,000 words is a good minimum for a mainstream novel and the first writer should confine himself to a maximum of 100,000 words except in genre like glitz where the baseline, as can be discovered at any bookstall, is probably 150,000 words minimum. However, for the established author (a class into which readers of this book are now moving) whose track record the publisher knows and from whom he may commission a book before much or anything of it is written, the advance is calculated as a percentage of the selling price multiplied by the expected number of copies to be sold – with the selling price to a goodly extent related to the thickness of the book. The number of words agreed on the contract is therefore a *minimum* below which the author should not fall; if the author is very well-established, and the book is not being produced to a tight pre-established format or price as many non-fiction books and some novels are, the publisher might even pray for a big surplus, because he will be able to put the book price up without increasing the advance. Apparently a book which will sell a certain number of copies will not sell more because the price is lowered or fewer because it is increased, given that these changes do not bring the price outside the broad range of current prices of similar books of approximately the same size. Strange as it may seem from an author who claims to be interested in the mechanics of publishing, I did not discover until recently that contracted wordages are usually minima; a quick telephone poll revealed that it was news to many other established writers as well: they take the 'about x words' in their contracts as maxima and, like me, call or write to their editors for permission to overshoot the mark or at least to apologise when they have irretrievably overshot. On the other hand, the publishers of this book intend the contracted wordage as an upper limit, for the simple reason that they are trying to produce the book to their renowned production standards but also to a price they believe you will find attractive and affordable.

Of course you already know about regional interest as an important factor in the marketing of many books, but did you know it may transcend national boundaries? This publisher had bought the British rights in my ice-race novel *Iditarod* on condition that he got the Canadian rights as well. The eponymous race is in Alaska, a territory that forms part of the American volume rights, but they expect a book on an ice-race to interest many Canadians as well and of course the race-publicity broadcast in the lower forty-eight States is available in every Canadian home as a TV-boost for this particular edition of my book. Now, I know about this broadcast spillover because in advertising I often worked with media-audience statistics, but how could another writer possibly find this out unless he had lived in Canada? And, if he knows, should he tell the publisher? Certainly not, unless he is an old pro, because the publisher will merely think a new writer impertinent. (And, despite my special knowledge, I didn't even think of Canada until my publisher reminded me of it; *he* told *me*.)

The answer, of course, is not to worry about these complications until they arise but to let it be known to your publishers that you are always open to suggestion, guidance and compromise. Write the book in the way that will best communicate your purpose, and then adjust it as necessary in the light of reasoned editorial input.

4
LET THERE BE ORDER
A PLOTTER'S COOKBOOK

ONE easy way of spotting the incompetent or careless teacher of writing is that he imputes to the plot of the narrative-in-planning a life of its own, and to the process of plotting an almost mystical importance. Whether these errors arise from stupidity, thoughtlessness or laziness is irrelevant to those whose writing careers they hurt; the result – mechanical, uninvolving writing – is always the same. Yet a moment's thought will convince any writer that the way to the reader's heart is through his involvement (jargon: identification) with the characters. Unless you can first touch base at the reader's heart, you cannot reach his mind or his purse. It is not a lack of good ideas or a failure of logic in arranging such ideas into perfectly sequential plots which causes so many writers to drop out after a book or two; the failure is caused by emphasising the purely mechanical aspect of the plot at the expense of the characters and the characterisation. The result, while perhaps entertaining in the same cold way as a *Times* crossword, fails to convince the reader that real people performed the actions in the book. The consequences are predictable: rejected or remaindered books.

Unfortunately, the wrong emphasis on plot to the exclusion of character is often more obvious in second and subsequent books. This is because a writer's first book or two are usually conceived in the hot flush of enthusiasm around an action of the main characters: character and action arise in the beginning writer's mind as a unity. It is an involuntary process. But the writer converting his talent into a profession, trying to repeat an earlier success by attempting consciously to plan a new book, all too easily, and quite involuntarily, shifts the emphasis from characters creating a plot to a plot jerking cardboard cut-outs around. A great deal of teaching in creative writing reinforces this entirely natural but disastrous tendency by promoting a critic's post-creation tool, plot analysis, as the primary pre-creation planning tool for the writer. You've heard of Parallax Error; well, this is Inversion Error, arguing from dissection by plot analysis to construction by plotting, which any pre-Structuralist logician will tell you is an abomination. Or you might consider that a story – a novel, a play, a film obviously but also in the better biographies, histories and other forms of creative narrative writing – by the nature of its dependence on the actions of people is not a mechanical construct but a biological growth. Any biologist at his dissecting table who pretends that he can reassemble a living frog from the sliced constituent parts can instantly be seen as a fraud – at best he can make the frog's leg jerk in a travesty of life, a cruel but precise analogy for the displacement of character by plot in bad books.

Plot is the servant of character. No exceptions.

Your actual plotting methods are irrelevant. My own books *Start Writing Today!* and *Writing a Thriller* and John Braine's *Writing a Novel* contain straightforward plotting methods, which may be summarised as 'write down as briefly as possible the chain of motivation that drives the characters to their actions'. I really cannot emphasise enough that the plot is not simply a list of things that happen: it should and must be a description of *why* people do things. If your plot merely lists events as actions in sequence over time, it becomes all too easy to invent characters to perform actions necessary only to the plot rather than essential to the character, with the predictable result that your readers remain unconvinced that your characters did indeed act as you claim they did. By contrast, the plot as a unified chain of motivation of your characters suggests the inevitable reaction of the characters to each action, and often surprises the writer by suggesting events that would not otherwise have occurred to him, events the reader believes implicitly because it is perfectly clear to him why the character acts as he does – the character can not do otherwise. The right attitude pays. The right attitude is that character is everything. Plot must there-fore stem from character. If you already understand this, there is no need to rush to my earlier books or Mr Braine's to pick up plotting methods: whatever method you use now will do, given only that it works, that it does not waste time, and that it concentrates on relating motivation to character as the driving force behind the cycle of actions and reactions through which you will tell your story.* That should take care of most plotting requirements most of the time. This chapter is therefore devoted to plotting problems probably rarely met by novices but likely to be encountered by the professional in proportion to the number of his books or years in the profession.

WRITING AS PLOTTING

Writing is not a neat process, so writing about writing cannot be tidily compartmentalised. Writing activities are not isolated either chronologically or conceptually from each other, so we should first consider the process of writing the actual narrative as an aspect of efficient plotting.

Writing is plotting It is a mistake to assume that before you start writing you must absolutely finish the plot with every possible event and detail to be included in the book. As long as your chain of motivation for major actions is clear and convincing from the written-down plot, you will not be punished for starting work on your book. On the contrary, you may be rewarded. Many (my own experience is most) plotting problems are best solved in the process of writing the book, or even disappear altogether once you start the narra-tive; it simply isn't worth wasting time agonising over them. It is for this reason that John Braine, for instance, advises

---

* Novices and aspirants reading this book are reminded that in this book we take the primacy of character as axiomatic for any professional writer. They should refer to *Start Writing Today!* for a detailed explanation of why character is supreme – understanding the reasons is quite as important as subscribing to the faith. In addi-tion they can save time and frustration by adopting someone else's proven plotting methods, whereas the writer primarily addressed in this book will already have worked out his own and need not waste time learning new ones.

that your final plot outline should be no more than two thousand words: that is ample to demonstrate the unified chain of motivation but leaves no space for confusing superfluities.

Write for show, cut for the money   Are you giving space to motivation/characterisation at the expense of pace? This question tortures many writers but that they ask it is almost always a signal that they have not started writing the book (or in the case of absolute novices that they have not finished their first book and started cutting it). It is a time-waster for professionals until one day they stumble over the solution, then it never bothers them again. The solution is to write for complete and exhaustive characterisation but to cut ruthlessly with your eye fixed unblinkingly on the pace of your narrative. That way you capture all possible events inspired by the character of your leading actors but can cut in the certain knowledge that the motivation behind the eliminated events will subtly illuminate the character in the remaining events. The reader does not expect you to tell him everything: what he expects is that *you should know everything but tell only what is relevant*. From that your reader will make closures* in his mind (a process that would repay investigation – we don't know enough even about the acceptance by readers of literary conventions). The character will glow and reverberate with the motivation and inter-character associations and frictions of the cut events, among other reasons because your writing in the remaining events will be so much more confident as a result of your own greater depth of knowledge of the character. Don't deny yourself any riches: write every event and scene revealing character. Don't deny your reader excitement by renouncing the pace appropriate

---

* This is a useful concept from the study by psychologists of perception. It describes the creation of a complete image from incompete data. Artists count on the fact that most people share the conventions by which their society perceives relationships between objects, persons and ideas. They have to, because the whole is often too complex for the artist to render; this is the rationale for symbols and referents in painting and poetry. In narrative prose these emotional, social and mechanical closures are aided by the literary conventions readers and writers hold in common, like the cutaway from a scene too harrowing to describe, so that the cutaway itself in the right context becomes a finger pointed at a harrowing experience. The context is itself a component of the closure.

to your material: cut *all* events and scenes which do not reveal *essential* aspects of character in *relevant* action. If you cut self-indulgently, this advice will not work, but those who do not learn to cut with the immovable rigour of a Puritan will in any event never become professionals; cutting is such an important art that Chapter 6 is devoted entirely to the gold you can pick up on the cutting-room floor.

THE PROFESSIONAL WRITER'S PLOT PROBLEMS

In the remainder of our discussion we shall make little distinction between plot problems you discover in the process of plotting and those you discover in the process of writing. Though one might at first think that these problems are less likely to strike the very practised writer, my own experience and that of other writers who tell me their troubles is that problems are problems, regardless of your experience, perhaps because creating a full-length narrative is such a godawfully complicated business that no-one can keep all the requirements and pitfalls constantly in mind. Provided you don't panic, however, experience has its uses: whenever you consider a given problem, sooner or later you will remember a related problem you have met before, together with a solution you can adapt.

The all-purpose nostrum   One writer, capitalising on his Nobel Prize, contracted for a book to be delivered in half the time he usually allowed himself. He did deliver on time, by the simple expedient of 'skipping all problems for the time being – you'd be surprised how many go away when you don't worry them'. Excepting two qualifications, to which we shall return, this is excellent advice, with the additional advantage that following it lessens the temptation to create a problem simply so that you can give up writing for the day. If you meet a problem, regardless of what it is, make a cross in the margin, or a note, and continue with the next paragraph or section. The simplest example is where you are short of a fact; breaking off to consult an encyclopedia or going to the library for deeper research can wreck your writing rhythm –

71

even checking the spelling of a word can put you off your stroke. (I have dictionaries on my wordprocessors that will stop me when a misspelt word is typed in but keep them switched off for precisely this reason. Doubtful words can be marked with a question mark or other symbol in brackets. Ditto for words where you need to consult a thesaurus for a reminder of that much more precise word on the tip of your tongue.)

Bigger problems often answer to the same remedy. Sections that seem dull and boring in the writing are very often discovered in the cutting and rewriting stages of the book to be quite unnecessary. If your writing is boring you it will certainly bore the reader. Stop, make a note that the section is incomplete, and continue with the next section. If you discover on reading the material later that something essential is missing and should have been included in the incomplete section, you then have the choice of completing the section, now a somewhat tastier task because it has a definite purpose and with the added incentive that when it is finished so will your book be, or of including the necessary information elsewhere and cutting the incomplete section altogether. My own experience is that sections which seem dull and dragging in the writing almost always prove to be scissors-fodder; their lack of excitement even in creation is your mind's way of warning you that they are unnecessary.

The first and lesser qualification to this trick is that it doesn't work with the names of your characters when they momentarily escape you. These small breaks in your work-flow can mount up substantially but there is a simple solution: keep a list of all character names beside your keyboard

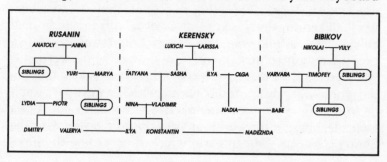

and refer to it instantly when you cannot remember a character's name. If you are writing a complicated work you might want to spend the time to make a graphic representation of the relationships between characters. That nearby is for the novel I am working on right now, *Dzerzhinsky Square*.

The other qualification is much more important. You must not skip a section or passage merely because you fear that for technical or emotive reasons it will be difficult or painful to write. A teacher of writing, seeing on my wordprocessor screen between paragraphs the note 'In here write torture scene', promptly demonstrated from two of my own published books that the torture scene I wrote in sequence in one book was far superior to the one I wrote out of sequence in another book. Shortly afterwards I had a similar experience with the draft of a friend's novel. I knew he had written one sex scene in sequence but baulked at another because of personal circumstances occurring at the time he should have written it; the sex scene he wrote out of sequence was very substantially inferior to the one written in sequence. Sex and violence aren't the only subjects that can cause problems. One biographer has difficulty writing action scenes (as opposed to 'background') but has now stopped putting them off until the end of her books because she realized that in telling a story chronologically she writes better if she does the bits difficult for her in the right chronological order – which would be ironic if it weren't so painful for her, because she finds it irrelevant to the quality of her work whether the background she writes so fluently is created in or out of sequence. She also notes that 'once you stop putting [troublesome] sections off and start writing them in place as a matter of habit, the edge of fear goes off them because you don't give it time to build up'.

There is a by-product of this solution to plotting problems that appeals to many writers: it helps you discover which items you should routinely leave out of your books because you are writing them not for yourself or for your readers but because you think some literary god expects them. As an example, I used to hate writing the detailed description of the surroundings of my characters which is still a feature of the 'serious novel'. Increasingly I left it to be written when I had finished the rest of the book, and when the time came I often didn't bother. Then I noticed that I skipped detailed descriptions of places in the books of other writers. Now I don't even mark the spots in my own books where I leave out such passages because I have no intention of ever writing them. That material was never an integral part of my style, and leaving it out has done me no harm with my readers and publishers; the critics who have noticed don't spend their own money buying books. (This doesn't mean I leave out all description, merely that I have discovered that the minimum relevant description, which flows from my keyboard as smoothly as action and almost without my noticing that I am writing description, is all that is required for the sort of books I like to read and write. It probably follows that I shouldn't accept a commission to write a travel book unless it focuses on people rather than places – which also describes the only kind of travel book I read for pleasure.) If you routinely leave something out to be written later and then discover that its absence does not detract from the completed book, it probably isn't necessary. These items announce themselves by being tiresome to write and boring to read rather than difficult or disturbing to write (and perhaps painful to read but a necessary catharsis all the same) as in those we have met above that are essential to your work.

Small pieces of paper Whether you follow my sub-division of parts of narrative (concept, theme, event) or some division of your own or none, the order of events can often give trouble in the planning stages. The advice given to novices, not to sweat the order at the plotting stage but to write all the scenes and then to shuffle, is good but owes more to the belief that novices extract most benefit from writing-writing-writing than to any intention of speeding completion of the aspirant's book. For the more experienced writer, trouble with the ordering of events in his plot signals either that he has more events than are required to explicate his theme or, more rarely, that he does not have enough. Too few events is no problem at all, because the chain of motivation will display an obvious gap or gaps which cannot be bridged by any combination or permutation of the available material; therefore the gap has to be filled by additional events, invented in fiction or researched for a non-fiction book. In addition to the chain of motivation being gap-toothed, the events to hand will also fail fully to explicate one or more of your themes, and this too should be obvious even to the relatively inexperienced. The two conditions do not in theory necessarily go hand in hand but I am not familiar with any example where they did not.

Note that the obverse is never true: logic tells us that if the chain of motivation is complete but a point you want to make is inadequately explicated, the point must be irrelevant to your narrative and therefore superfluous. Another way of saying this is that only those themes are essential to your story that can be illustrated by the shortest possible chain of motivation which is true to your characters. Writers who cannot resist making detours should stick to the established form for those with taste for digression: the essay.

Too many events is a trickier problem. The novice has to write them all because he doesn't command the experience to decide which are superfluous. The writer with a book or two behind him has a better chance of eliminating superfluous events without first writing them. This is done by shuffling events into the shortest possible chain of motivation: those that are not required for the chain of motivation, either because they are at a tangent to it or duplicate a motivation already illustrated in another event, can be dropped. In this regard it helps if you write your two or three line descriptions of events on three-by-five cards or strips of paper, rather than trying to write the whole thing out cohesively on a single sheet of paper; cards or strips of paper are easier to shuffle or to lay out on your desk in various combinations and orders. Which event(s) to drop is an easy decision: you keep the most dramatic ones, the ones you can use most easily to impress the author's authority (especially early in the book), and the ones where the facts are least likely to be known by readers. Some writers have other requirements. Since most of my books are pretty hefty, I would normally, all other things being equal, prefer the event that when written will be shorter. 'Dramatic' takes care of choosing events in which action features over those containing only exposition. I also have a preference for the visual and the visceral over the cerebral. It is as well when you are stuck with a plot-sequence problem to give thought, once more, to the total image you want to leave with the reader at the end of the book. If you know precisely what you want the reader to think, you can use the desired end product as a measure against which to weigh the contribution of each event.

Climaxes first　In a mystery novel it is obvious that the denouement is the climax and all other scenes are arranged to lead up to it while creating the maximum tension. But in most other genres, including the modern thriller, very frequently there is a number of events any one of which may be chosen equally convincingly as the climax. This also applies to much non-fiction, with the added complication of a known chronology of events. Once more, recourse to your cards or strips of paper will show which arrangement is preferable to all others. However, resist the temptation to arrange climaxes in an ascending slope from the smallest to the highest as this sort of artificiality is easily spotted and grates on even unsophisticated readers; also it can make the beginning of your book dull and give an unfair impression in the opening pages of a lack of excitement, losing readers you would have retained with a better considered arrangement. I have been irritated by obviously artificially arranged plots so often that now I deliberately check that mine do not have any kind of a geometric arrangement of climaxes; if one happens by accident, I destroy it by additional shuffling or, should that prove impossible, by removing an entire key scene to the beginning of the book as a prologue. One editor who reads substantial parts of around four hundred novels a year has a term for artificially pyramidical plots: he calls them 'salami-slicers'.

It is in any event a good idea to open the book with a bang, especially if you can use the bang as the impetus that triggers your chain of motivation. If you cannot arrange your events to put a bang first, and will not invent an event especially for an opening bang because that will ruin the balance of your story, you can always offer the reader a partial, 'teaser' preview of some climactic event to follow much later in the book. In the Andrew McCoy thriller *The Meyersco Helix* the reader discovers right at the beginning that the president has three minutes to decide whether he will nuke Boston or let a deadly self-regenerating water-borne poison spread across the world – and is then held in suspense for several hundred pages before he discovers why the awesome choice is put before the president.

From thesis via antithesis to synthesis   The book of ideas, without much action, whether fiction or non-fiction, is very tricky to arrange so that it doesn't read 'flat'. The ideal is to set up the ideas in the form of a statement and counter-state-ment, a format which holds its own friction, and then to create tension between the writer and the reader based on the reader's doubt whether the writer will bring off the resolution of opposites. It is for this reason that so many heavy readers, faced with a book that for professional reasons they cannot put down before the end, groan when they discover the writer opens with his conclusions; if that is the best bang the writer can offer, he should save it for his climax rather than throw away half the tension of his book by such a clumsy arrangement. The opening bang must raise questions for the reader and the only conclusions that do so are controversial ones. The shortcoming of controversy is that today's heresy is tomorrow's orthodoxy – and in an ever-shortening cycle, which limits the useful life of a book which relies on contro-versy for its opening bang.

In fiction, history and biography, thesis-antithesis-synthesis is also a good format for giving the bad hats the benefit of the doubt or a voice to speak in. Ian Grey's *Stalin*, for instance, almost makes one believe that Stalin had no choice but to murder millions, yet achieves this feat without ever making one doubt the good sense or compassionate nature of the author. Mr Grey does this by observing the times from a Russian viewpoint, setting up Stalin versus his competitors, and letting the power of terror resolve matters; it is a trick, of course, but the reader has to stop himself thinking, If such methods were good enough for Peter the Great and Ivan the Terrible, why not for Stalin?

Thesis-antithesis-synthesis is also a useful tool for discovering whether there is a gap in your understanding of your leading character(s). A biographer must see world cataclysms through the eyes and morality of the boy Dwight growing up in Abilene at the turn of the century or he will make no sense of the actions of the conqueror Eisenhower. This is not as easy to do as to suggest: in many respects the historical phenomenon of Stalin's Russia is much more accessible to us than the private world of Abilene all those years ago. However, if those East Coast writers whose Eisenhower biographies fail to satisfy had bothered to look behind what they saw as knee-jerk military-mind reactions to events, and to give Eisenhower the benefit of thought, a balance of statement and counter-statement would surely have shown them a deficit: they would have discovered that they did not know why Eisenhower reacted as he did and in the ensuing search for the missing motivation might well have discovered the importance of Abilene.

Unfortunately thesis-antithesis-synthesis has its own downside. It deals in abstracts that are often difficult to interpret (in the paragraph above the morality of individuals and states is an easy choice) and may be impossible to translate convincingly into discrete and manageable events; for purely practical reasons the popular historian may prefer to start from observed action and search backwards for motivation. This doesn't stop a really clear thinker, Paul Johnson for instance, from working from the abstract to the manifestation (with chapter heads like 'The Devils', he might prefer 'infestation') but we should not pretend it is an easy option. The precondition is that you should understand your material so well, and in history and biography have digested all events so thoroughly, that you can draw general conclusions and build your book outwards from the chain of motivation suggested by the general conclusions, selecting your events to suit; this obviously describes only the highest level of writing by the best minds. The main disadvantage is the ease with which this format can become pompous and overbearing, especially if the weight of what you have to say does not match up to the formality of the structure. In fiction, it works for those occasions where the writer sees no evil but only unfortunate circumstances (disaster novels, for instance) and it is good for giving the black hats a chance to show their viewpoint; but when there are real bad guys it always seems like a shoddy trick played on the reader when the baddies get their comeuppance. Also, it works only for serious fiction, dealing in serious issues, making the author of less weighty material appropriating it appear like a pompous, pretentious hypocrite.

Duck's Disease   A film executive who told a writer that despite having a feature script in his hand he didn't have a film was unable to point to any gap in the chain of motivation (in film jargon, every action was justified by having its causes 'established'): the story was apparently complete but he didn't think people would want to go see it. 'It just doesn't taste right in the mouth. I want something more but I can't tell you what it is.' And again: 'A duck,' said another film executive challenged to explain what was lacking in an apparently fully motivated script, 'is an animal with serious height shortfall. Its ass is too close to the ground. Everyone knows it except the duck. Nobody knows why it is so. No one can do anything about it except the duck, who can walk on tiptoe or get elevator webs.'

Most writers with a few years of experience have at one time or another felt that there was something serious lacking in a project without being able to put their finger on it. It appears to be one of those problems which answers better to empirical experience than analysis. The likelihood seems high, to me at least, that the writer didn't truly identify with the leading character. If so, can he really expect readers/viewers to identify with the character? Of course not. Talking to writers in this bind, one hears complaints such as 'While I like the character, there is still a certain distance between us. But what is it? What causes it? What can I do to narrow it?'

The writer feels that in a just world the cause should have shown up glaringly on the common film analysis and planning tool of the outline in master scene synopses, the paradigm of the narrative writer's chain of motivation – but the chain appeared complete and closed.

In prose narratives, which are normally much more complicated than a film, such an indeterminate shortfall in understanding and projection can be much more frustrating, in part because there are more facets of the story to consider.

First, resist the temptation to create more events in the hope that they will somehow solve your problem; you will be sorry when you discover you wasted time writing events you later have to cut. If every point in the chain of motivation is adequately explicated by one or more events already in your plot, the gap must be in the chain of motivation. At this point there is usually in classroom situations a tense exchange that starts with: 'But you distinctly told us that events relate to and flow only from the chain of motivation. Therefore, if the chain of motivation is complete, an event must be missing. You can't have it both ways.' True, writers and teachers can't have it both ways, but the chain of motivation can: it is easy for the chain of motivation to seem complete and internally consistent but all the same to leave you with the feeling you have two hours after a Chinese meal: something missing. The reason is that you haven't fully understood your character(s) and that they are still holding something back from you – and, therefore, from your eventual readers. No understanding, no conviction, no writer or reader identification with the character. Film people, who are only too aware that they spend millions in a time-frame that can present no more than the essence of a character, seem to be more instantly sensitive to this problem than writers for other media. (The other reason filmmakers are sensitive to incomplete characterisation is because what they most want from writers is a star vehicle which will attract a bankable star – and stars like to play simpatico characters.)

When you succeed in fully plumbing your character the link missing from your chain of motivation will be obvious and you can then add an event to illuminate it in action.

For the historian and the biographer this problem is a lot easier to solve than for the novelist: you need further careful consideration of the available material, giving yourself time and peace to accept new insights, and further research if all else fails. It can take a great deal of frustrating time because you don't really know what you're looking for, only that you are searching for something that will round out the character for you. It is little consolation that this knowledge of something amiss, almost a sixth sense, is the beginning of true professionalism. However, you must follow it through to the bitter end, until you discover what is lacking to complete your character and his story. Once more, a good example is the way in which an absent or incomplete understanding of Eisenhower's Abilene childhood marks those of his biographers who fail to convince. In fairness it must be said that in a life like Eisenhower's the early Abilene years constitute spatially such a minor part of the story as almost to disappear in the rest of the pageant; only the inspired and persistent writer, or the one fortunate enough to share a similar background, will grasp their disproportionate influence. This example illustrates how difficult it is to discover what is missing when your chain of motivation seems comprehensive yet your command of your character is somehow inadequate: how could a Boston-bred brahmin ever discover the missing small-town mid-America link whose absence makes his Eisenhower biography read like a condemnatory tract? The answer is simple: he was never well enough in sympathy with his character to appreciate his motivations; *he should have trusted his instinct,* the taste in his mouth, that he didn't quite understand Eisenhower and waited until he did or chosen another subject he understood better.

The fictionalist appears at first to be in a good position to patch up such a shortfall in his understanding of a character. After all, he invented the character: he can now modify him to suit. But the writer's mind does not work like that. Characters mutate in the subconscious to spring into being almost full-grown. They are just there, one day, all of a sudden. What the novelist actually does is to develop them from there, which is not the same thing by a long chalk as modifying them to suit his predefined purposes. At the stage of creation under discussion here, we already have a list of events inspired by the character's known characteristics and don't want to duplicate any of those, so the question is not what the character will do but which facet of his character is as yet unknown to the writer and therefore unilluminated by action. My own quick fix is to switch into Blackmail Mode: What is this character's guilty secret? What does he fear most? (This one is also good for knowing how a character speaks – I don't know why but it works.) Basil Zaharoff, the arms pedlar and one of the most colourful characters who ever lived, was dead on the pages in the early drafts of *The Zaharoff Commission* until it came to me that he had a church burned and a politician killed to prevent the fact of his illegitimate birth from becoming known not so much because he craved respectability for himself but to protect the Spanish duchess he loved. These events and the duchess herself receive altogether a half-dozen lines in the book and those lines strictly in passing – but the influence of the insight (right or wrong is another matter; Zaharoff's only credible biographer makes much of the man's quest for respectability) on everything else I wrote is what made the difference between merely an exciting thriller and a convincing historical novel. It was, if you like, the final breakthrough to his character. No additional events were created to account for it but several were modified in the light of my better understanding of his character that resulted from the insight: these are the scenes most often remarked on by editors and readers, the scenes with a high 'stickitivity index'.

Tone of voice as a control on the unknown   Since this kind of vague feeling that you have not plumbed the full depth of a character either in non-fiction or a novel can usually only be resolved by spending a great deal of additional time with your material, and since some time might pass even after you discover a solution before you recognise it as *the* solution, it is often wise to start writing and to use the tone of voice of the narrative as a control. You know the right tone of voice instinctively: it suits the material. Everything else feels awkward, tailored for a smaller person. The tone of voice will not feel right until you have fully plumbed at least your chief characters. I knew that my little insight to Zaharoff, a man of many secrets, was the right one because immediately afterwards the tone of my writing started fitting the action and characters like an old glove. Once you discover the correct tone of voice, you should scrap what you have written and start again at the beginning to ensure that both style and characterisation are consistent throughout the book.

...with a gun in his hand   Stuck for what your character does next or says next? Switch viewpoints for a moment to see if seeing the event from another character's vantage doesn't jar something loose.

Stuck for a motivation for the character to do something you want in the book? Put it in, as long as it isn't anything major, and let the character explain he is doing the unexpected to confuse his enemies or just for fun or because he always wanted to.

On a more serious note, when stuck always remember that randomness and unpredictability are consitituents of the human condition. Anything too rigidly planned casts a chill over the reader. People in real life are not perfectly predictable and neither should characters in books be. But also remember that they are normally reasonably consistent in all the bigger and more important things.

And, if all else fails, you can always take Raymond Chandler's advice to let a man come through the door with a gun in his hand.

PRAY SIR, FOR WHOM DO YOU PRÉCIS?

Summaries of the chain of motivation and its resulting events differ according to when in the process of creation they are assembled and for whose use they are intended. It is worth defining our terms because the words synopsis, outline and proposal are used loosely and interchangeably in publishing and the broadcast media and in addition may mean different things in books and film work.

First, a **proposal** is what it claims to be, an offer to create a work hopefully of art but failing that at least of persuasion or entertainment. We shall investigate an example below but the format can be anything from a piece of self-laudatory prose to a detailed analysis of the market for the work. The length and content can be whatever the writer thinks will best convey his message and get him a commission. It might also include an outline.

An **outline** is a description of the intention of a proposed work of art and the methods by which it will be achieved, sometimes including a detailed, ordered description of the chain of motivation and the resulting events; the amount of detail included depends on the purpose to which the outline will be put and by whom. A special form of outline in use in the film industry is called the **outline in master scene synopses**; this is a consecutively numbered, exhaustive compilation of very brief descriptions of all events to be included, the purpose of the whole being to demonstrate that the chain of motivation and action is unified and complete.

A **synopsis** is a summary of a work already created or to be created. It is normally intended to demonstrate the chain of motivation and resulting events of a narrative, and may be used to decide whether the subject matter is suitable for a particular medium or to the taste of a publisher or producer. Synopses are made either by the creator of a work of art or entertainment or by readers employed by producers and publishers; those made by readers for film producers are almost invariably more detailed and of better quality than those made by readers for book publishers; the quality of a synopsis by the original creator depends on his experience and honesty. A pure synopsis is a very hard thing to find in a trade that deals so largely in opinion.

A **reader's report** is a synopsis of content accompanied by an opinion on the suitability of the material for publication or production by a particular publisher or producer. If the material is judged publishable/producible 'but not for/by us' the writer might be sent a letter advising him to 'try So–and–so instead.' Sometimes the reader's report is called an evaluation; in film circles it is often called a synopsis.

A minimum fiction proposal   The length and detail of proposals and outlines depend more on the relationship between the writer and publisher or producer than on anything else. Overleaf you will find the proposal from which the publisher commissioned *Dzerzhinsky Square*. This is the complete proposal; there is nothing more to it, no outline, not even my phone number because the publisher knows it. The publisher did ask me for two more sheets, proposing two companion novels, because he wanted to commission a trilogy. They follow the illustrated format so exactly that it is not worth giving them a page each here.

It is worth analysing this near-minimum proposal in some detail, not for its format but for its intentions. It is addressed to a publisher who has previously commissioned half a dozen books from me and bought subsidiary rights in others from the commissioning publishers; he does not need convincing that I can expand a one-page, or for that matter one-line, concept to a novel. However, while it is ostensibly addressed to him, and kept short enough not to waste his time by telling him what he already knows, it is *aimed* at the other parties on his various decision-making committees, who may not know me even by reputation (senior staff in publishing now change around almost as frequently as in advertising at the height of the rat race), and in particular at the sales and marketing departments. For them it does three things. It tells them the subject; because they sell books by genre they want to know up front that the subject is saleable. It impresses my authority on them by a selection of esoteric detail both small and large, chosen for no other logic than dramatic impact and memorability; remember that your piece of paper may be distributed in advance to be quickly read by someone with many other demands on his time and it does not help you if in the meeting he confuses your proposal with another. Finally, it gives both publisher and marketing people something to handle, to wave around, to prod their memories, to use as a place-holder in a scheduling file; for this latter reason, even if a publisher tells me at the lunch where I pull

DZERZHINSKY SQUARE
by André Jute

Lubianka was an insurance company whose headquarters building Feliks Dzerzhinsky's Cheka took over for office space. It is still inhabited by the highest officials of the KGB because it is more convenient to the Kremlin than their huge modern offices seventeen miles from the town centre on the Moscow Ring Road. There is an inner courtyard, backed by another building containing, among other things, the torture and execution cells (not in the cellar of the main building, as often claimed). The main building has green linoleum on the floors; the execution cells out back are said to have had rubber mats on the floors to catch the blood. The street side of No 2 Dzerzhinsky Square is painted olive-green, with white facings to the window surrounds. The front door is guarded by two members of the élite First Kremlin Guards Division, the ones with the double red tabs to their lapels. They look across the square to the world's largest department store, GUM, and, incongruously, to the world's largest toy store, Detsky Mir (Our World). They can also see the onion domes of St Basil's and the Clock Tower near the Spassky Gate to the Kremlin, just along from Lenin's Mausoleum. The Lubianka is a centre of power, and power has been wielded from it from the very beginning of the Revolution; Dzerzhinsky moved here from the Smolny Institute in Petrograd immediately Lenin transplanted his revolution and capital to Moscow.

Our story, nothing less than the sweep of humans (and inhumans), inquisitors and victims, who make up the history of the KGB from its beginnings as the Cheka in the Smolny, will be told in the first person by three generations of KGB officers: the Extraordinary Commission from the beginning – and from the inside, motivated by its own imperatives of fear and fanaticism, through the murders of whole professional classes, the massacres of the kulaks, the betrayals of friends and family, the show trials of colleagues, the psychiatric tortures of dissidents, right up to glasnost, when the fourth generation must answer the question, Was the result worth the effort?

The story will abound with real characters, the great, the mad, the lethal, even the chill technocrats, from Lenin to Stalin to Beria to Chebrikov. The historical detail will of course be impeccable. And the tension, the tragedy, the final ray of hope and humanity in the realisation that oppression cannot work forever, all is inherent in the material.

- 200,000 words. The material will support a novel of 250,000 words if considered desirable.

the idea out of the air that the book is in the bag, I would write something down and send it to him. (It is also relevant that the contracts people in many publishing houses like to be reassured by the editorial staff that they have 'something in writing' though in Britain they probably never ask to see it or I would long since have had a demand from some outraged contracts department for something a little more legally binding than a couple of paragraphs on a single sheet. American legal departments are much more likely to want to make the proposal and outline a part of the contract.)

This is still not a minimum proposal. The whole of the penultimate paragraph is, given the material and my track record with this publisher, self-evident and superfluous. You cannot write about the Russian secret police over this stretch of time without including the great and the bad straight out of history; rigorously researched historical detail has been a feature of many of my novels and the publishing director would be insulted if I considered it necessary to remind him of it. It is however more than simple self-promotion, something that too many writers shrink from. Salesmen of books like to think they toil, however humbly, in the fields of literature; your editor knows you will not sell quality down the river but it is worth reassuring the sales department that you will offer them a product they can be proud of, and that is what this paragraph aims to do.

If I were approaching a publisher who has not published me before with a detailed outline, I would still use something very much like the illustrated proposal as a cover sheet. It is unwise in business to assume that any presentation will be read thoroughly or that uninterrupted attention will survive the first five hundred words, which corresponds to a page of single-space typing; the safe assumption is that you must hit your target in the first hundred words at least to the extent of providing a mnemonic to which to tie your name and proposal when your turn arrives in a meeting at some later stage.

The minimum non-fiction proposal   Even the most minimal non-fiction proposal should describe the subject, the scope of the treatment, the intended market, and something startling either by way of novel fact or whatever it is in your approach which will differentiate your book from all others on the same subject. Even on a single-page proposal I like to meet the scope-description requirement by offering the chapter heads, with second heads where they are not explicit (as for instance in this book); this is the fastest and most economical way of showing the ground to be covered, information absolutely essential to the publisher in determining the appeal of the book. Many creative writing instructors tell you to leave market-determination to the publisher but my experience is that publishers appreciate authors who understand that books have to be sold. To know the nature of the market and how big it is – and who else competes in it with what goods and how effectively – demonstrates professional awareness of the publisher's operating-space, which in turn engenders belief on the part of the publisher in the writer's abilities.

Generally speaking, you should not put intended price or production information in the proposal – unless it is essential. For instance, I have a proposal for a technical book on colour print reproduction where the only competition is outrageously expensive but where I have discovered an electronic production method that can cut the in-store price by two-thirds. Of course this is relevant information, even essential; without it the proposal makes no sense. It is self-evident that books intended for students should be produced down to a price and only an idiot would run the risk of offending a publisher by stating it, but in some markets your information about the purchasing power of potential buyers is probably superior to that of publishers and then you must not blush to speak up. When I started writing for other writers, it seemed to me that big, turgid books missed the mark because most aspirants could not afford them; six years later books for writers are generally more modestly priced, so perhaps publishers have learned.

The outline   A good outline is far easier to write than a salesmanlike proposal, because you are not so cramped for space and because the specialist task the outline must perform is perfectly familiar to every serious writer: demonstrating a unified chain of motivation and action. There are three ways to present an outline:

- as continuous prose to leave an impressionistic taste of the finished article with the reader

- broken down by key set pieces (fiction, biography, history) or topics, in either case perhaps with subheads

- as a comprehensive listing of every event or non-fiction point, perhaps even numbered in order as in the outline by master scene synopses

Which you choose is a matter of temperament rather than skill, with some consideration of which medium you are working in and who you are addressing – some formats are obviously better suited than others to communicating with those who require more detail from you. In addition, it seems that different kinds of material impose their own requirements on the format of the outline, something that had not occurred to me until for this book I tried to rewrite an existing outline into the alternative formats.

The prose outline An American publisher asked through my agent for an idea for a novel, then that I should expand the proposal to a series; he specified each outline should run to about 8–10 pages. Overleaf you'll find the opening for the outline of the second proposed book, done in an impressionistic narrative style.

The cover page gives a taste of the subject material and makes it clear this is a thriller. The outline jumps straight into the hero's guilty secret, the driving motivation behind this story, his desire to stay alive; this as good as tells the editor I consider character vitally important. Bradley is introduced in a character-revealing way and so is Kerensky, a main character, plus the point of the story, the plane. Later we will discover all is not that simple... but any publishing executive who has time to read only this far will grasp that because we

THE OSAKA STING
by André Jute

**THE PROBLEM WITH THE JAPANESE IS THAT THEY TAKE
THEMSELVES SO SERIOUSLY.
BUT THEN THEY HAVE PLENTY TO BE SERIOUS ABOUT.**

**INCLUDING THE WORLD'S ONLY FIGHTER PURSUIT
PLANE FITTED WITH A RADAR THAT CAN DETECT THE
FEARED STEALTH BOMBER WHICH NO ONE BELIEVES THE
PRESIDENT HAS PUT IN MOTHBALLS.**

ESPECIALLY NOT THE RUSSIANS.

'Soon you'll be so bored,' says the voice behind Bradley just loudly
enough to give him a heart attack, 'you'll start selling the Pavilion to
wealthy American tourists.'

Ben Bradley sits on the beach, leading the life of a rich loafer. The
problem is that he sits on Brighton Beach, below the bulbuous Pavilion
built by the Prince Regent in 1806. Which was also the last time
anything, anything at all, never mind exciting, happened in Brighton
(unless you count the invasion of the local fish-and-chips shops by the
Teddy Boys in 1957, three years before Bradley was born – they broke
a shop window, which to Brighton is still a big talking point but to
Bradley, an American hardened to the excesses of real Hell's Angels,
Californian variety, is very tame and very distant indeed). And the
reason Bradley, who has millions, is caged on boring Brighton Beach is
that the intelligence services of virtually every nation big enough to have
one, plus some freelance assassins and plain terrorists and other guns-
for-hire, are scouring the more fashionable beaches along the Med for
him. Bradley had, a little ambitiously it must be admitted, stolen his
millions from them. And when they find him they intend to see him
dead, though not immediately: his slow, painful demise will serve as a
warning to others. 'There is no such thing as a free lunch,' said Milt
Friedman, who was one of Bradley's heroes, but Bradley had never
imagined that a little lateral thinking and American go-getting would
leave him no alternatives but to be bored to death or to be tortured to
death. Bradley, who between Harvard Business School and perforce, to
save his life, becoming the biggest conman of all time, had been tried
and found too lateral-thinking for corporate conformity by the three
Generals (Foods, Motors and Dynamics), felt guilty all the time, not
because he had ripped off all these people (they had been trying to kill
him) but because he had been inculcated with the work ethic – and now
he was idle.

The man who has nearly given Bradley a thrombosis is the elegant
and cultured blond KGB mover and shaker Kerensky, executive side-
kick to the sinister Kurusov, the Great Russian Survivor. He has a deal
to offer. Bradley impressed Moscow at the time of the Ferney-Voltaire
affair when he ripped off their money for the plans of a flanged monster
field-gun he had already sold to the Indians – and actually escaped with
his life. Now the Russians want something: a high-performance
Swedish SAAB prototype fighter pursuit plane on test in Japan. The
Russians want Bradley to steal the plane.

have a character we have a story, and every film executive will know we have a star vehicle. The minor detail and the direct attack on the material has stamped my authority on it in even that small space, something that will not escape power-breakfasters. The consequence is that, if the decision-makers are interrupted at this point, they can in good conscience scrawl 'OK' on the corner of the authorisation memo and pass it back to the commissioning editor who will open negotiations with your agent to develop the project. Executives who have not read the outline by the time of the meeting can skim this far and be hooked. The art is to give them the least possible opportunity to say no. Notice that the writing is fairly entertaining (in fact, this is the second draft; the first outline was returned with a request that I make it less funny – British publishers have a much better sense of humour than their American counterparts, except on the subject of advances). That the writing should represent what you will offer in the book is especially important when you are dealing with executives who are not necessarily familiar with your style, and that's virtually all the time, given the ebb and flow of staff.

A sample of writing obviously related fairly closely to what will be in the book itself also saves you the frustration, sometimes met when you do a detailed but dry-as-dust event by event outline, of the publisher complaining that 'I know what you're going to say, but not how you will say it,' followed by a demand for a sample chapter, which is an insult to an established author and, in fiction to my certain knowledge but probably also in the more thoughtful branches of history and biography, a disrupting residual influence on the later creation of the complete book. These chapters written to nudge the publisher's imagination almost always have to be thrown away and replaced by something else because in the writing the book mutates; if you use them as they are or with patching, the joins always show. Having a chapter or section you wrote to satisfy yourself the project is a runner is a different matter; whether you can show it depends on how much polishing it requires. Since my own trial pieces are always very rough, they take as much time to smooth down as to write something entirely new. The whole business of showing part-work is a pain, especially since the publishers most likely to demand it are invariably those with the least capability of understanding where you will go from there – it is their lack of imagination that instigates their demand for a sample – and the greatest propensity for dumb suggestions. Not one of the editors who have made really innovative contributions to my fiction or non-fiction have ever asked for a sample of a projected book. A quick phone-around among the literary tax exiles in the green and beloved isle persuades me this is general wisdom; many of the wealthier writers prefer not to do commissioned books because of the frustration of explaining subtle concepts to less subtle minds.

Among the other advantages of the prose outline is that its method does not come between the author and his material, and that the material shapes the presentation.

Set pieces   The prose outline does not necessarily include every event you plan to put in the book, though it could. But it should certainly include all the key scenes. In fact, a useful method is to introduce the character(s) briefly and then to say outright 'And here are a few set pieces', after which you list them, each with a brief description. This lays bare the major motivation without having to oil each link, and also displays the structural integrity of your book, the connection between the major climaxes, without too much camouflaging minor detail. It is an easy study for the kind of editor you expect to contribute something to your book, because he can see almost at a glance (we are probably considering eight or ten double-spaced pages) what should be added, subtracted or moved for maximum persuasion; if what you are writing is opinion, it is normally also clear where your emphasis will fall, so that from the exposed structure he can track the main lines of your intended argument.

In non-fiction your material will fall naturally into back-ground information essential to interpreting the action of the characters and foreground events. Even if your outline is complete, many publishers will ask for a list of chapters and topics as well because they are accustomed to visualising books that way, so it is worth including even if superfluous to your own purposes. Another advantage of this simple format is that it instantly shows where you need to apply additional effort if your chain of motivation and event is incomplete. I always make a list of chapter heads and topics for non-fiction books even when the outline is only for my own use; sooner or later it will come in handy and then you don't have to hunt up your notes and spend hours picking your way through them and a prolix prose outline to do what is only an hour's work in its proper place.

The outline for this chapter is a minimal but perfectly clear example taken from the proposal as approved by the publisher of this book.

---

4. A Plotter's Cookbook

When the evergreen methods fail, try these. Tricks of the trade to unglue sticky plots. Hurdles that are actually warnings. The minimum workable outline for the writer v. the minimum workable outline for the publisher to show the sales manager. The danger of overblown outlines, the importance of leaving something fresh to discover in the actual writing. Starting with a bang. Breaks, flashbacks, fugues, rhythm; importing formats from other media. Mechanical and commercial implications for creativity in the selection of endings.

The outline in master scene synopses This is primarily a film-planning and analysis device but many writers, including a large number whose attitude to films and film people is 'take the money and run', swear by it for planning any kind of complicated book. Its great advantage is that it confers a virtual guarantee, excluding only an outbreak of Duck's Disease, that you will achieve an exhaustive and perfectly ordered chain of motivation and action – and with less effort than the innocent might believe.

An outline in master scene synopses is created by listing *every* event and its motivation in order. The film version normally includes a heading indicating whether the location is in or out of doors, the place and the time of day.

Some writers dislike the numbers but they are part of the

---

31. INT. JACK'S SITTING-ROOM. MORNING.
Dave and Marian argue bitterly. Dave is appalled at the violence of his reaction. He cannot trust himself not to strike her and storms out.

32. EXT. CARPORT/STREET. MORNING.
Dave, his face contorted with rage, on the verge of tears, jumps in his car and roars away down the street.

---

format. In using this format to plan prose fiction you could combine both these events under one number, 31, and dispense with the heading; I find, however, that if I stick to the accepted format as if for film the visual impact in the reader's mind of the resulting prose is much enhanced.

The advantages of this planning format include making both gaps and redundancies in motivation and action instantly obvious. On the other hand, an outline in master scene synopses offered to anyone but film producers must normally be accompanied by either a sample section of prose or some explanation of how you will present the material. Says one publisher, 'Subject matter is important but, unless the subject matter is unique, I am much more interested in the writer's attitude to it, the approach he will take in actually writing the book. The more often I have worked with a writer or the longer his track record with other publishers, the more likely I am to take his command of the material for granted and the more heavily his approach weighs in my decision. If a writer comes to me with two projects, unless one is so much more appealing to the marketing department on subject matter alone than the other that the choice makes itself, it is probably a foregone conclusion that I will choose to go with the proposal the writer himself is more enthusiastic about. Enthusiasm translates into extra sales.'

The treatment for film There is a another format in which an outline for film can be created: a sort of mini-novel. This is written like any other prose outline but at greater length because more minor events must be included; it makes sense to attempt to include all events because film producers are so keenly attuned to even minor gaps in motivation, the sort of thing that even the most pernickety book editor will take on faith. (Some writers think film people lack imagination but this is a misconception; film producers have a different kind of imagination, shaped by different aims and pressures and conventions.) Since many films are mooted and developed some little way but few are made, you should try to salvage something besides the cheque from a commission to write an original screen treatment. There seems to be no accepted 'correct' length for a screen treatment: those commissioned from me have almost always come with a request for 'about thirty thousand words' but other writers report producers asking for lengths as low as ten thousand words and up to 'about novella length'. However, there is no harm in asking if rather than the producer's preferred length you may instead write the treatment as a novella and retain the volume rights in it; no reasonable producer will refuse such a request and if the film does get made you will have the 'book of the film' directly to hand for a nice bonus. If, as is more likely, the film is not made, or the television series dies in the pilot, at least you have a book you can flog for extra cash.

The screen treatment created from an existing literary property is merely an expanded synopsis. More often than not its main aim is to delete all the superfluous actions, motivations, subplots and characters from the book on which it is based. Sometimes new material has to be invented to make it acceptable to the star on whose name the film will be bankrolled. Otherwise it is written like any other synopsis.

The synopsis and the reader's report Where a publisher or producer asks you for a synopsis of an unwritten book, give him a proposal and outline in any of the formats discussed above. A synopsis of a completed book is merely a précis, as you learned to write at school and university, and should demonstrate the unity of motivation and action, or otherwise, of the work. A reader's report is a synopsis with an opinion added as to the suitability of the work for some purpose.

If a book publisher asks for a synopsis of a complete book, give him one single-spaced page that contains the subject matter, a quick summary of the narrative progression, and something by which to judge your approach or whatever else is unique about your book. If a film producer asks for a synopsis, give him anything up to twenty pages which should include every event essential to the minimum chain of motivation and exclude every event superfluous to it.

Once you are well established as a writer, there is no reason you should not refuse to supply synopses of complete books and films; your earlier published/produced works are the publisher's or producer's guarantee that he will not waste his time reading your work. I normally forestall the request, and the unpleasantness of refusal, by accompanying all manuscripts with prepared text for the blurb on the dust jacket front flap, and all scripts with a cover page containing an extended version of the sort of come-on you see on posters outside cinemas. Here are a couple of script examples:

For a serious political film

In 1952
in the last titanic struggle for the soul of America
one man has the vision and the power
to do what has to be done

Harry Luce can do his patriotic duty
– and destroy his friend

Or Harry can be loyal to his friend
– and betray his country

Which would you choose?

And for a police procedural

Jake Oliver embarrasses the new FBI.
So they put him on the first plane out.
To team up with Moscow's only honest cop.
Against the KGB – and the CIA.

The blurb instantly allows the publisher/producer to see whether my conception of the book/film corresponds with the kind of book/film he likes to publish/produce; it also serves as self-promotion for me and as a benchmark for any alternative promotion the marketing people may write – if their blurb is inferior to mine, I raise hell. Most writers have the skill to do this but some lack the chutzpah.

Writing by the numbers of the plot   Don't. Even when you have marked up the numbers yourself, forcing yourself to write by them is bound to create prose that reads like an artificial insemination manual. If in the writing you discover a better way of presenting the same concept or motivation, do it. Even in cases where you have a commission and where you are contractually bound to the agreed outline, no publisher in his right mind will force you to follow it if your alternative version is demonstrably superior (given, of course, that you haven't turned a book about searching for the yeti into a discourse on carrot crops in Tahiti or something equally unreasonable). You may observe that the finished chapter you are now reading bears more than a passing resemblance to the outline shown earlier but is certainly not a slavish mirror-image. For instance, to avoid wasting space through repetition I have included material that theoretically should fall in a later chapter; I have also shuffled some of the material around and shifted the emphasis because that now seems to make better sense; furthermore, some minor and not-so-minor bits and bobs have been lost and/or replaced with other bits and bobs that seem on deeper reflection to be more important. None of this is important enough to call the publisher and discuss the changes; I expect no query. The novel *Dzerzhinsky Square*, under construction concurrently with this book, differs from the proposal printed above in that I discovered in early drafts that telling the story of three families in the promised first person would be tiresomely choppy for readers, and therefore decided to switch about between characters in god's-eye view; in addition, as a binding device, I created a fourth major character not even mentioned in the proposal. These could if you were so minded be considered major changes and, if I were doing the book for an American publisher (who belongs to a breed much more legalistically attached to the agreed outline), I might call and attempt to explain why I have made them; but the book is for a British publisher with whom I have worked for fifteen years and I suspect he would rather I didn't waste his time with long explanations about an alteration that is, at least with hindsight, inevitable, and which in any event does not change the main thrust of the novel.

The parts that overplots don't refresh   Overly detailed plots destroy initiative and joy in your craft. Writing is a hard slog and one way it is enlivened is when one of your characters does something unexpected, which usually allows you to discover an amusing plot twist. Or a character might make a crack that raises a smile on the face of his creator. Even the smallest discovery helps lighten the grind. But you will discover nothing small or large if your plot is too detailed and you follow it slavishly. Your characters will be like cell mates of twenty years standing: dull, boring, known too intimately, people with no secrets. It doesn't take much experience for a writer to recognise another writer who plots too closely: it shows in his writing, which reflects the drag he finds creation. Leave yourself something fresh to discover every day in the writing.

If your publisher is one of those who want to plumb all the depths of a story before he commissions it, tell him where to get off, find another publisher, or write the book on spec. My greatest disasters were all created for an otherwise extremely lovable publisher who absolutely insisted on having 'an outline of at least three thousand words'. As a result I spent too much time with the characters in the plotting stages: when it came to the writing I was so bored with them that I resented every word dragged onto the page in those books long before I had spent the last of the generous advance. Readers don't resent reading your dull words, they just stop.

THE PERILS OF PAULINE

We have already commented in passing on the shape of the narrative, most notably in the sections about climaxes and starting the book with a dramatic event. These are obvious matters that require no great emphasis when speaking to writers with a book or two behind them, but it is worth even a professional author's while to consider tension in greater depth than the obvious elements of the arrangement of climaxes, or as a means of signalling to your reader right at the beginning that you fully intend to satisfy his craving for excitement.

A touchable intangible   Tension is the element that keeps your readers reading. They want to know what happens next. The reason they want to know what happens next is because you have involved them with your characters. They care. In the classroom we might say they identify with the characters. Stop and think what it means: they feel joy and pain when the character does. They do not read on for your glittering description of the fireworks, but to discover if the character escapes burning.

Unfortunately, you cannot plot for tension. The basic concept contains potential for tension: you would not write the book if you did not believe people would want to read it. The situations and events of the story contain potential for tension, especially if correctly juxtaposed. But while some classroom gurus, who will never see commercial publication, stop there, these are in fact only the most superficial and least valuable of a writer's tensioning devices.

From our belief that tension arises out of reader identification with the character, it follows that tension is built primarily in the process of writing the narrative. You can't expect the reader to identify with the character unless you have first presented the character for identification, and that you can do only in writing the book.

At nine Mr Byng was shot   We have already met the opening bang as a promise to the reader that grabs him like a door-to-door salesman and drags him into the narrative. But it serves the additional purpose of introducing the character in relevant action, putting down a marker on the reader's emotions through what may be several expository sections of background material or scene-setting until the character reappears or again does something exciting.

The opening bang should, for commercial reasons, have its own opening bang. Potential readers in libraries and bookstores often open books at the first page; you should apply your first paragraph to grabbing the sale or the loan.

The barb   Very few books are read at a sitting; most people put them down at the natural break between sections or chapters reached nearest their bedtime. Even fewer have a consistent level of excitement throughout. If the reader's bedtime should arrive at the break after a dull section, your book might not be picked up again – and if that happens too often your next book won't sell. It is good practice to end each section, but especially the dull ones, with some more or less blatant promise to your reader. 'In the end, oil killed an American city.' This line from my novel *Sinkhole* falls at the end of the opening bang and is followed by several sections of much less exciting though necessary scene-setting in an average mid-Western city. Since there is a requirement to demonstrate peace and tranquillity to contrast with events after the disaster, the characters are introduced in everyday, read 'dull', action. The reader reads on because he has been offered an IOU of action to follow. The hope is that the line, and the promise, sticks in his mind like a burr on a saddle-blanket until the action picks up again. The copy-editor who cut the immortal barb 'Soon we shall be able to square the circle,' from the end of a chapter only specialists could love in a friend's book of high mathematical philosophy will surely burn for her insensivity and lack of humour.

Meanwhile back at the ranch   This is a hoary old chestnut of unputdownability yet the intention is not only valid but, considering how much tougher the competition for publication and readers is today than in Zane Grey's heyday, crucial.

'To Harry Maxim it seemed as if his wife died twice.' I don't care how long past midnight the reader opens Gavin Lyall's *The Secret Servant*, I will bet money that after reading that line he can't put it down until he has discovered what Harry Maxim felt, what he did about it, what *happened*. It is a hook, defined as the first line after a break (any break, even just a line space), designed to draw the reader into the section by his need to answer the question posed for him by the line: who, why, where, what, how, when?

I shan't insult you with a large selection of barbs and hooks; you will find enough in the work of the writers you love and you would in any event be better employed devising your own than studying those of your peers. But I cannot resist printing my favourite brainchild: '12.06p.m. For the first time in her life she regretted her agnosticism.' Anyone who isn't compelled to discover the cause of such a volte-face is simply not civilised. A hook is an excuse not to put the cat out just yet.

Breaks Your plot or topic-list imposes certain logical breaks but within and without the sections dictated by logic there are other opportunities occasioned by breaks. Many academic writers like sections to be short, fictionalists seem today to tend in the opposite direction. But the length of your sections proves nothing: why not let the material dictate them? Furthermore, what purpose does a breakdown into chapters serve if the chapters carry merely numbers without titles – won't a line space indicate your change of pace or subject equally well? Once you get rid of artificial and mean-ingless breaks imposed on literature by the lost tradition of reading books aloud after dinner, you can then apply the breaks to their best purpose: building tension. A mere line-space before the climax can heighten tension much like the blackout for the commercial break on television on those occasions when there are no commercials and the screen fades right back up into the action. Don't overdo it to the extent that it becomes obvious as a trick. Against this, some writers believe that exciting sections should appear to continue forever without offering the reader relief, wringing him out with the maximum possible amount of action.

Huge chunks of dull but necessary exposition can be given the appearance of forward motion, and therefore tension, by inserting breaks at changes of subject or approach, if necessary at much smaller changes than cause a break in more exciting stuff elsewhere in the book. In non-fiction your choice of subheads, their rhythm and their placement, may all be applied to motion and tension. If all else fails, try reducing the text and substituting *relevant* pictures; even if you join me in not believing that a picture is worth ten thousand words, it is amazing how much a good photograph accompanied by a well-written, extended caption can convey.

Rhythm   Tension is enhanced by occasional relaxation. This is one reason why the pyramid of climaxes one sometimes hears about in classrooms is such a stupid objective for practising writers. The tensioning-relaxation rhythm should pick up towards the end of the book, with a shorter cycle. If you can't manage that with the plot as written by you or by history, can you take out some dull stuff and turn it into an epilogue falling after the climax, where readers can choose to give it a miss? Many biographies of great men would be vastly improved by hiding their declining years in a space where the general reader can ignore it but where it is still available to scholars and students forced to drink the cup to the dregs. We shall return to the subject of natural climaxes below.

Watch out that you don't create a chopped-salami cycle of tension-building action alternated with absolutely equal-length sections of more relaxing matter; that too irritates with its artificiality. Don't worry about it overmuch in the writing but do make a point in the rewriting and cutting stages of checking that you haven't fallen into this trap.

Flashbacks   A flashback is the depiction, either in real time from a god's-eye view or in some character's memory-time from his own viewpoint (not necessarily first person), of an event that happened earlier. It can be used to alter narrative rhythm or directly to build tension. The watchword is subtlety. Professional writers will of course rewrite rather than position something out of sequence simply because they forgot it earlier. Clumsily *placed* flashbacks make the same incompetent impression as material included as an afterthought; in addition clumsily *introduced* flashbacks look like shady tricks and lose you the reader's confidence. Never announce a flashback. 'He remembered how it was when...' is not only clumsy but it is a man remembering rather than a flashback, which must be action experienced in its own time and place rather than mere nostalgia, however concrete. A line space is all the break you need, then straight into the action; you can indicate a different time and place by the context. If you are really confident and skilled (try Jerome Weidman's *The Sound of Bow Bells* for a masterful display) you can switch into flashback mode without any break.

The fugue   A useful transition device, not limited merely to flashbacks but especially helpful with them, is the fugue (pronounced fewg, one syllable, not few-gew, two syllables, whatever you may hear television directors say). This is not a movement in funeral music but a connecting link between two scenes otherwise apparently unrelated. The cliché fugue in film is the unseen telephone being heard ringing in one scene and observed to be answered in the next scene; technically it is a sound-bite carry-over link. In fiction and non-fiction prose it can be anything: a smell, the colour of the mud on the river where an old general fishes which exactly matches the mud of the river where he suffered his greatest defeat, the curve of a woman's breast, the hawked hook of a man's nose seen on a bus, merely a word in the barb at the end of one sentence repeated in the hook at the beginning of the next section – whatever provides the reader with a sense, not necessarily conscious, of continuity.

The flashforward   In his novel *The Color of Light* William Goldman uses the fugue of a meeting of the children of alcoholics to flash his character forward several years to... another meeting of the children of alcoholics. He does it right in the middle of a paragraph and never returns to explain what happened in those years. This is in any event the finest novel (so far – Mr Goldman is still a relatively young man as novelists go) by an entertaining writer but it is worth seeking out simply to study this one item of masterful technique. Why bother with the dull years of a character when you can lose them in the middle of a sentence? Not incidentally at all, the character in Mr Goldman's novel is a writer – and I know no professional writer who doesn't have a feeling of lost or wasted years somewhere in his life.

Inspired larceny   We have already met the outline in master scene synopses, the fugue, and other artefacts from the visual media recommended as tools to prose writers, and some prose tools recommended to film writers, but it is worth explicitly stating the premise: if a tool from another trade looks useful, appropriate it. Don't worry if professors of literature will not recognise it as a literary artefact: you are not writing for them; this is between you and your readers and you should grab everything you can that will smooth communication and comprehension. For myself, I have also pillaged psychology and economics and computers and advertising for tools, but only because I know them; you must have specialised knowledge in some field that can provide models or tools if only you open your mind to them. A tool any writer brings into the trade becomes common property.

The End

There are mechanical, creative and commercial implications in your selection and/or arrangement of material, especially obvious in relation to endings. The division between the implications are not always clear but that is not important except when mechanical or commercial considerations cause structural problems that bring creative frustration in their wake.

The life and times of Richard M Nixon   Let us suppose four writers each have a contract for a book on ex-President Nixon, all with the same publisher. There are already enough general biographies, including a steady seller from this particular publisher which these books should complement, so each writer will concentrate on his speciality as related to Mr Nixon's career. Respectable scholarship is taken for granted but the publisher is keen for a good sale to the general public as well.

Writer A is interested in domestic policy. He would be well advised to make his climax the resignation and pardon by President Ford, and should then as a winding-down chapter for the general reader turn to how the pardon crippled the Ford presidency, signalling that additional chapters on Mr Nixon's later years, including his attempt to unify the Grand Old Party, need be read only by scholars and specialists. There is no great excitement here and general readers could, unless the writer lets them off the dull bits, form their whole opinion of the book from what they read last. One solution is to open the book with Mr Nixon at the 1980 Republican convention, taking as a concept the residual power, or the lack of it, of a man so long at the centre of political life; at the beginning this could be given an excitement which, by contrast with everything else, it will lack at the end of the book.

Writer B is a specialist in foreign policy. He has a problem: at a point, which he is capable of assessing accurately, Mr Nixon became so involved in the Watergate debacle that foreign policy was largely determined by Dr Kissinger. He can step lightly over the rest of the Nixon presidency to the resignation and pardon. But his climax is in the next chapter: the aftereffects of the Nixon policies; for instance the final outcome of Nixon's kitchen debate with Khrushchev almost thirty years later in Mikhail Gorbachev's perestroika, Nixon's recognition of China turning it into a more responsible member of the international community, and a whole raft of other important matters. If I were doing this book, I would try very hard to persuade the publisher to let me end the book there, without any description whatsoever of Mr Nixon's later years, which are entirely irrelevant to the continuing influence on international affairs of his actions when in power.

Writer C is a student of the fourth estate. His study of Mr Nixon's relations with the press will reach a sustained climax with Watergate, the resignation and the pardon. Again, he would be well advised to signal to non-specialist readers that the rest of the interplay between Mr Nixon and the media is of lesser interest; alternatively he could work the post-Watergate material into an earlier chapter so that the pardon is the final event in his structure.

Writer D will place Mr Nixon in context as an American phenomenon, tracing his psychological make-up from his poor childhood through the first fierce campaigns and the communist scares, and proceeding through the late and luke-warm endorsement by Eisenhower at the time of the 'Checkers Affair' to the 1960 Californian gubernatorial election and thence to the presidency and Watergate. But this writer can place his own main analytical contribution after the pardon, when for the first time Mr Nixon had time to reflect. The recounting might proceed from the standpoint that though it does not behove him to say so, Mr Nixon, a keen student of American politics, cannot be unaware that objectively the Kennedys were the most efficient American political thugs of this century, making Teddy Roosevelt look like a would-be bully too stupid to harness the awesome power of the state against his enemies and far surpassing Boss Tweed as purveyors of patronage. Yet the supposedly liberal media broke Nixon, an exemplar of the American dream, for much lesser crimes against morality than those of Bobby and Jack Kennedy, who by contrast where almost deified. Does Mr Nixon feel the pardon was necessary, or did he accept it to protect the office and the institution from further attack? How does a man cast from the pinnacle reconstruct his life? The climax may be the resignation but the resolution is the point where Mr Nixon comes to terms with his history. The writer can easily arrange matters so that the resolution is in the very last line of a chapter in which his analysis places his subject squarely into the twentieth-century American psyche. In a sense, this writer says, You may think you know the facts, but here is the real truth. Unless handled clumsily, that obviously creates a continuing tension by the interest it generates with the reader. It is a more difficult job than the other three hypothetical projects but proportionately more rewarding and important.

'Literature is tragedy'   This is errant nonsense, an unwarrantable inference from the observable but not exhaustive generality that most of the classics are tragedies. A tragedy is a book that displays the price to be paid by the Good for the defeat of Evil, or for the failure of the Good to be good.

The misconception has implications for writers. Tragedies get a better deal at the hands of the critics than any other prose, and the same goes for literary prize juries. (When did you last hear of a genuinely funny book being awarded a major prize?) Even failed attempts at tragedy earn the writer brownie points merely for trying, which leads to a great deal of overblown trash being created and often lauded beyond its merits. By contrast, the literary establishment is very likely indeed to look down on any kind of narrative with a 'happy ending' as 'mere entertainment'. Most of these critics' darlings and 'award-fodder' writers have tiny readerships and huge bottom drawers full of unpublished manuscripts while the purveyors of happy endings fill the shelves in bookstores.

The implication is that if you have the right material, and the skill to handle genuine tragedy, you should not deny yourself a shot at the glittering prizes; if your book is honest and true it will find an audience.

However, if your material is merely pseudo-tragic, why deny readers the happy ending they crave? If you don't, all you will get is slack sales and worthless praise – readers have a sharp nose for the insincere and the critics you respect won't be taken in either.

As a specific example of the choice facing the writer, Andrew McCoy is convinced that if he had somehow contrived for the revolutionary Jomo Iningwe to live at the end of *The Insurrectionist* the story would have been less well received by critics and made less impact with readers.

But his agent says sourly, 'A lot of readers rooted for that character and were disgusted when the author killed him. They won't buy his next book. Also, you can't turn a dead hero into a series.' There, in a nutshell, is the decision you have to make.

5
THE ANSWER TO EVERYTHING
STRENGTH OF CHARACTER

EVEN if you have never consciously subscribed to the doctrine of primacy of character, by the time you have cut and rewritten two books to your own satisfaction or, better still, that of a competent editor, you will have subsumed a large part of the wisdom that an understanding of character is the root of all effective narrative and the cure for most narrative ills. We have canvassed some of the reasons in earlier chapters and there is an extensive introductory discussion in the companion volume to this book, *Start Writing Today!* The reasons are important enough for the professional writer to consider consciously but any intelligent writer with a little experience can deduce them from his own tribulations at his typewriter and the evidence of books he admires; self-instruction is, as always, the practising writer's most valuable tool.

Purpose, mystery and mechanism We have until now taken it for granted that the character is your emotive link with your reader and that the character is best presented in relevant action. We know very little in any scientific sense of why this should be so, but that is not quite as important to the practising writer as to the literary exoskeleton of academics and critics; no space will be spent here on speculation beyond that necessary to clarify practical methods. That does not however mean that any mystique should be attached to the link between literary character and flesh-and-blood reader; resist the temptation to think of it as a black art and substitute instead the down-to-earth attitude appropriate to evaluating an operator's manual for a professional communicator's toolkit. Mystery is of course a thing of beauty but you are the creator of that beauty and it will be cheapened if you are yourself baffled by it; the writer is an interpreter, and the reader has the right to an interpretation that does not abdicate its responsibilities in a cloud of pretentious incomprehension.

In that spirit, this chapter therefore approaches character (which as always includes 'characterisation') as a tool you can use to make your meaning clearer to your readers and to solve most of the problems a writer meets in his work. As a practising writer you may, and should, be familiar with most of the tools and methods described in this chapter, even if you have never consciously recognised them before; the ideal is that you should recognise each tool, either from your own work or your reading here, and be astounded and delighted to discover what *else* it can do for you – if you are constantly writing, this chapter should help you solve a problem or two very shortly.

CREATING MEMORABLE CHARACTERS

In analytical discussion, the criterion for the perfect character – perfect in the sense of being affective and therefore credible – is that he should 'develop'. This is an unfortunate definition, conjuring up nothing so readily as otiose or etiolated persons well into middle age still 'searching for the real me'. We all know from everyday observation that a real person's character by the age of thirty-five has achieved the immutability of a fly in amber – and will not change short of being shattered with a hammer. More: thirty-five is an outer limit because character-formation slows down from puberty onwards, and after the break between education and entry into work proceeds at a snail's pace.

However, the novel is *novel* in the sense that it is about a unique event, or it is a *romance*, which implies that a generally agreed level of improbability will be tolerated or even welcomed as an escape from the reader's own less-than-perfect reality. In biography the assumption is that the book would not be written or read unless it is about an uncommon character or one with some other claim on the reader's attention arising from his unusual circumstances. In history the unusual and impactful event is highlighted, resulting in a narrative that is different from a novel or biography only in perspective and choice of facts. (This assumes that the events are presented as the actions and reactions of characters, which is not always the case, as any remaindered or unpublished history will prove.) What all the narrative formats in successful creative writing have in common is that they deal with the uncommon. It is in this sense that we must grasp 'the developing character', because the context of the narrative describes the large environmental, physiological or psychological change to which he must adapt to survive. I prefer the description 'memorable characters' because that relates more precisely to both the writer's and the reader's perspectives on characters.

To the writer, characters are interesting in relation to their external circumstances or their internal balances and changes or the conjunction of both; if a character's circumstances and environment are dull and matched by a dull mind, no one wants to read about him and you would not want to write about him except to make a point, perhaps about his hypocrisy ('Once a month he rolled up his sleeves and washed all the way up to his elbows.') as a representative of his time and place. To your readers, the character is interesting in so far as his circumstances and environment open up new vistas or his thought processes and adaptations ring a bell of truth or provide hitherto unconceived perspectives. The reader wants vicarious experience – and most definitely not of the kind he can get at his own kitchen sink, which is why the kitchen sink novel failed nowhere so badly as with the class it depicts but was read by a small coterie of socially-responsive Hampsteaders and Georgetowners who caught a vicarious thrill from their concern for the less fortunate. Whatever the emotive content, the more uncommon it is, and the higher the writer can reasonably and convincingly pitch the affective link with his reader, the longer the reader remembers the character. Andrew McCoy has spoken to many readers who agree with his agent that he betrayed them by killing the character they were rooting for, Jomo Iningwe, at the end of *The Insurrectionist*. Since this is a novel of serious politics and the moral that violence will have to be paid for is clear throughout, these readers are not making a rational point based on the author's facts but an emotive response based on their identification with the character he created. It might be instructive to try reconstructing your own emotions on finishing *Moby Dick*. We are not constructing an argument for easy endings that let the reader off lightly – on the contrary, that would probably dilute the memorability of these books – but adducing evidence that the easily grasped concept of memorability is a better test of good characters than the considerably more obscure concept of 'development'. If you read the better critics you will soon notice that, when they get down to the nitty-gritty, the aspects of any writer's work they appreciate most are precisely those characteristics that would help one remember a real-life character: pointed dialogue, the small peculiarity of dress or demeanour, a quirk of circumstance or mindset, the unexpected flash of wit. If it is good enough for such jaded but discriminating readers it must be good enough for any writer.

The word 'development' has one great advantage to offset its conceptual shortcomings: it clearly implies that there must be change, and that the change must be motivated by events. It is a convention of the novel, and a necessary condition of the uniqueness and scale of the events described in the other creative narrative formats, that characters will change consequent and in proportion to the events described. This is why the novel that purports to be nothing more than a description of everyday events creates in the reader nothing more than bored resignation; it is why the inexperienced and those with dull lives do not publish autobiographies and attract no biographers; it is why the best histories are about periods of philosophical or physical upheaval rather than about uneventful and therefore unexciting peaceful interludes. This is the most important aspect of the plot, that for maximum excitement and memorability it should set up or feature those events which provide the greatest and most appropriate impetus to character-change.

One more general point: since your whole story is perceived by your reader through your characters, your main concern at all stages should be to discover and illuminate character. You research with character in mind, you plot with character in mind, you write with character in mind, you cut and rewrite with character in mind, you précis and sell with character in mind. One of the most rigorous historians writing today is unmoved by compliments on the depth of his research: 'The facts are constant; discovering them is simply perspiration. What people do is merely the surface. Why they do it is always the meat of the matter.'

The memorable character develops   Given our discussion of terminology, you might consider this a tautology but it is not. No one is more boring than the character you can present instantly, Athena springing full-grown from the head of Zeus. Interesting people have secrets you learn slowly, peeling the onion of their characters. If you discover a character in your book is boring, have you perhaps revealed him too fully too early? Can you go back and hide something to be revealed later? Facts or events in the wrong place always feel more or less irrelevant, and often show a forced fit as if the writer stuffed them in there because he didn't know where else to put them. Furthermore, you might deliberate on the developing character, in the paced uncovering of his secret being, as a fine tension-building device – and write accordingly.

The memorable character is rounded   The well-made novel is best defined as one which leaves no questions unanswered in the reader's mind (John Braine is good on this: cf p132 of *Writing a Novel*); the same applies to non-fiction to an even greater extent in that such books are written to illuminate darkness or to satisfy curiosity. It follows that in both fiction and creative non-fiction all the major characters must be complete. That does not mean instantly on their first intro-

113

duction. The rounding is a process. However, you must hold faith with your reader by telling him everything relevant about the character at each stage of the narrative; he will reward you by his belief that you will in due course tell him everything else he needs to know. The unpeeling of the onion and the rounding of the character should ideally both reach fulfilment in the very last line of the book but, as we have seen, in novels that may be difficult and in non-fiction it is often impossible without throwing scholarly restraint to the wind. In the interest of tension you should seek a place as late as possible in your narrative to enter the rounding-out material; if you cannot do so without slowing the story use it after the main climax rather than leaving it out altogether. The concluding page of *Roots of Violence*, quoted below in another connection, falls well after the main and secondary climaxes and is ostensibly concerned with the revenge of a slave girl on a cruel master. But it also rounds out the two main characters, Lance and Esmeralda, by illustrating how their relationship to each other has been shifted in a small but significant way by their experiences: Esmeralda, whom we have been shown several times to be perfectly in tune with her husband, is no longer quite so much instinctively considerate of his reactions. This is an example of a very small change but much smaller and more subtle examples abound in all classes of literature; after forty years as an avid reader, I have come to the reluctant conclusion that in rounding off the character there is no objective size: the smallest *necessary* thing in its absence will ruin your book as effectively as the largest.

Roundness is an important tool to measure your work against if you wish to avoid succumbing to Duck's Disease, the inexplicable shortfall in a chief character. If he is not rounded, if he does not do what the chain of events has motivated him to do or, worse, if he does things for external reasons the likelihood that he will 'not taste right in the mouth' must be very large. In our earlier Eisenhower examples 'external reasons' intruded because the writers thought their subject was politically ignorant, unsophisticated or even malignant when the true internal reason for his actions was

the morality formed by his Abilene childhood. This particular example is one with an inherent extra danger for the
writer, in that politically committed publishers are not hard
to find. The problem of Duck's Disease is proportionately
much more serious in genres other than political biography
and in films is always fatal; apply the measuring tool of
roundness ever more stringently as you approach the top of
the entertainment ladder.

The memorable character is solid This is consistency, the
gel of the parts of character as you expose and stir them in.
What you require from this tool is for a red light to flash
insistently when a perfect blend is achieved so that you can
take the mix off the stove – and throw it out! You don't want
any Colonel Blimps in your novel, and if you have any in
your non-fiction the likelihood is high that you have misun-
derstood them, perhaps by not delving deeply enough. Even
for minor characters some very human inconsistency is desirable, if only to protect your back from rampaging critics or
junior editors trying to make a name for themselves with the
easy target of 'cardboard characters'; it is also easier to make
your minor characters memorable, a prerequisite of literature, if you do not make them boring, which is inescapable if
they are too consistent.

The memorable character is human People have quirks.
Their reaction to motivational impacts will on the whole be
consistent but no one is one hundred per cent predictable –
how terminally boring that would be! This is very difficult
because what your character does must never be unmotivated – that will destroy your reader's faith in you as the
presenter of a round and consistent character – but must
surprise and flatter by an unpredicted act that in the next
moment is seen to be fully motivated and in character. If your
reader is instead flabbergasted by being unable to relate the
action to what he knows of the character, you have lost him,
and probably not just for this book. What makes this even
more difficult to detect is that your agent and editor are not
reliable barometers: they are both jaded readers and there-

fore likely to inspect any reasonably well-motivated excitement with far less critical attention than they should. For the
paying public 'reasonably well-motivated' is never enough,
and uncomfortably often coincides with 'unmotivated';
perhaps this is because they get more involved with the characters than an agent or editor has time to do.

In *Start Writing Today!* I held up *Mrs Thatcher's
Revolution* by Peter Jenkins as an exemplar of a writer thoroughly at ease with his subject, pointing out that lesser
writers would start not with her motivation but with her
birth over a grocer's shop. As it happens, Hugo Young, who
starts his rival biography, *One of Us*, with the statement that
'Margaret Thatcher was born to be a politician', is not for
that reason a lesser writer. However, because he is so obviously partisan his book is both less convincing to the uncommitted outsider and less useful to the scholar than it might
otherwise be. On the other hand, because of precisely the
same partisanship coupled to a crusty Balliol style, his
spiteful narrative makes most amusing reading. Spite in an
author's work is often advance warning of a lack of understanding of his subject. Mr Young promises to explain to us
the stages by which Mrs Thatcher, who was once both objectively and in her own terms the ultimate outsider, became in
a dozen years the epitome of the British, in her own eyes as
well as those of everyone else. The key event on which all
other stages pivot is her defeat of Edward Heath, the
previous leader of the Conservative Party. Mr Young sets up
this event by painting her as the compleat ministerial mouse,
head down so hard to the tedious detail of an administra-
tively demanding department that her eyebrows clear the
ramparts of ideology only once in the previous two decades;
as far as it goes, this is very probably an historically
correct picture. And then the mouse commits the ultimate
Conservative crime, challenging not only the leader but the
whole ethos of the aristocratic party in which she is a lower-
bourgeois interloper! Mr Young offers a few limp guesses at
her motivation for this crucial event – his own lack of conviction is evident from his piling up of minor possibilities
without centre or focus – and right there destroys his book

because he fails to deal with his subject's motivation at a key juncture in her life. How could Mr Young possibly have failed to understand that to risk destruction is the paradigm of a turning point? The reader, even when history tells him that the outer form of what Mr Young describes actually happened, is astounded and confused by Mrs Thatcher's action and infuriated at the biographer for failing to clarify her inner motivations. After this display of powerlessness before his subject's most crucial life-changing choice, how can you trust Mr Young on anything else, even when he is apparently fully informed and superficially convincing?

There are enough Young-minded partisans of this particular subject and innocent lovers of stylish political bitchery to make this book a success at the cash register. But most biographies that fail on such a crucial point of motivation cannot be so lucky: they will fail commercially as well. One must assume that Mr Young genuinely intended more than to line his pockets, that he aimed to persuade the uncommitted that Mrs Thatcher was a dangerous woman; it is also noteworthy that the book was published by the family house of Harold Macmillan, estwhile prime minister, who is second only to Edward Heath in the Thatcher demonology of those who sold capitalism at the pass and who in his old age was an outspoken and influential critic of what she had done with his party and the country. Yet the book must be judged a failure because such an important missing link in the chain of motivation will cause any potential convert to withdraw confidence from the other conclusions.

Let's consider another historical but equally incredible political action that does convince because the storyteller gets it right. In Harrison E. Salisbury's *Black Night, White Snow* the most amazing event occurs when Kerensky, the leader of the Provisional Government, climbed into a borrowed car and drove away 'into the dustbin of history', thus guaranteeing the success of the Bolshevik Revolution; the succession was sealed when later the same day the mob took the Winter Palace. The reader is first stunned, then remembers that, despite Mr Salisbury's sometimes grim determination to be even-handed, Kerensky has consistently appeared as a

117

poodlefaker more given to the dramatic gesture than to effective, consistent work. A few years after first reading Mr Salisbury's account of the Russian Revolution, I had occasion to read several Kerensky biographies and then, in the same week, to reread *Black Night, White Snow*. This time I read straight through the Kerensky departure and it was only several pages later that I remembered my astonishment on first encountering this episode: having so recently been so deeply engaged with Kerensky, the stagy stupidity of what he did seemed almost natural! Mr Salisbury, by an economical but judicious selection of earlier events, has positioned Kerensky where his own reader can reach the same conclusion as the one who has struggled through all the learned tomes. Mr Salisbury has rounded Kerensky: he has made him a credible human being.

The memorable character reverberates   If you have ever cut a small novel out of a large one you will understand instantly what we are discussing here. What happens when you corral a shorter novel out of the proliferating plots of a big one is that characters sparkle with the subsumed, often even unmentioned, associations and frictions with other characters that were described in material now discarded. A generator offstage lights up a globe behind the eyes of the character on the page. The character reverberates (Shirley Young first gave me the concept and the phrase) with that unaccountable electricity in precisely the way a real person in crisis comes with a history and a background that the crisis-helper glimpses only obliquely but that have a major influence on the trend of recovery; the reader grasps the analogy and soon grows especially fond of the characters in books created like this. For instance, I cut *Festival* from a big, otherwise unsaleable novel about the arts in Australia; it consisted merely of the thriller subplot, which I rewrote for consistency. I would be the last to pretend that this somewhat plot-heavy collection of one-liners (I really enjoyed re-writing that book, it was so easy) is among my best but certainly the characters are better loved by readers I have spoken to in libraries and at literary luncheons than many of the characters from my far more 'important' novels; and film and television interest is also greater. The reason characters in such a novel make so great an impact is that the writer has the confidence of their other existence supporting them when he writes. The reader is soon aware that there is more to such characters than appears on the surface.

Of course it would be foolish to write long novels with superfluous action created merely to be cut so that your characters may enjoy residual electricity. But once you accept the benefits of reverberation it costs nothing to keep in mind that your characters have lives beyond the crisis-point where your readers meet them, and will have again once the crisis is resolved at the end of the book. This is the point where readers putting the book back on the shelf must feel the frisson of regret analogous to waving from the pier to an emigrating friend; the reader must want the character to return and the only way of ensuring this is if he feels there is something about the character still worth discovering. (Several of our other requirements and tools rule that this 'something' must not be anything essential withheld from the present story.) No one feels this tender about a character who has a life only within the story.

There is no need for you to write down the character's life external to the story. Such extraneous details arise unbidden during the thinking time every author must have; and if you do not deliberately expel them, enough will remain. Several years after publication of *Festival* I was asked for a few plot and continuity thumbnails by a television producer who could not make up his mind whether he wanted to make a telefeature (a full-length film), a teleseries (complete plot in each episode), a teleserial (plot plays out in finite number of episodes), or a series-serial (infinitely renewable plot, soap-opera). I was still so well versed in these characters' lives that, never even opening the book, in a couple of hours I dictated over a hundred possible plots they could be involved in. Sadly, far from being able to promise the same performance for any of my 'major' novels written before I had this insight, I would have to look up the names of the characters.

Unfortunately the effect of reverberation can be studied in

the work of other writers only by accident. Take Richard Condon's three *Prizzi* tales and, without checking the publication dates, read them in chronological order of events depicted. Then consider that they were published out of chronological order and it soon becomes clear that the two written later have benefited from Mr Condon's greater familiarity with the characters. The alternative, that Mr Condon – after a generation as a justly acclaimed novelist – had a sudden skill-breakthrough, is simply too risible for consideration. Or consider the work of Charles McCarry, who had written three distinguished novels about the poet-spy Paul Christopher before creating *The Better Angels,* set in the future and peopled with characters who featured as children in the earlier books; this book was an even better novel than the first three. But the best was yet to come. *The Last Supper* brings all these characters together in a novel ranging from the years immediately after the First World War to the eighties. It is superior in scope and execution to the previous novels, which were already outstanding in their own right. It is futile to ascribe this magnitude of improvement from such an elevated base merely, or even in large measure, to Mr McCarry's increased skill with passing years or practice with each succeeding book: the only possible explanation is the accumulation of greater insight into his characters.

The memorable character changes subtly Though we have agreed that if there is no need for your character to change over the timespan covered by your narrative, you don't have a book (and most especially not a novel), there is no literary or other requirement that the change be large. On the contrary, it must be proportionate to the event(s) motivating the change. The best books, with the most memorable characters, can present change very subtly indeed; try the agonised and agonising Russians for examples. But subtlety is not a requirement, merely what the civil service calls an advisory. After demonstrating in *Writing a Thriller* that Le Carré allows his character George Smiley, by not picking up a lighter when a defecting spy deliberately drops it, to reject the unfaithful wife Smiley originally gave the lighter to, I received a lot of complaints from aspirants who considered the example well out of their reach. That's nonsense: any kind of decent, thought-about writing contains many similar subtleties – and I could point to some of equal impact (if not so masterfully placed) in the writings of the wailing nellies themselves. All that is required is to keep your perspective right to the end and not be panicked by the requirement for change. Once you have the calm perspective earned by thorough familiarity with your characters, attention to the mechanical detail of your chain of motivation will automatically bring in its train the necessary creative balance, and you can count on routine cutting and rewriting to refine the balance further.

The perceived difficulties inherent in subtlety are however increased because the modern trend favours understating change rather than overstating it. This is a function of increased reader sophistication and the writer should take it into account by erring on the side of caution. But do keep in mind that this is a commercial consideration rather than a fundamental creative barrier.

How can you test your work against this requirement for change, and use the tool of subtlety? Perhaps the easiest measure of the change required is to evaluate the violence of events in the narrative and then to redirect the character's life accordingly; the method will always be arbitrary but at least conscious consideration improves your chances of getting it right, and of course you will improve with practice. In violence of event you should include both physical and psychological violence; don't forget that there are other kinds of violence, such as environmental and political violence, which can touch characters very directly.

As for subtlety, consider the violence a character commits in an attempt after some kind of upheaval to restore the previous status quo, and how he is forced to adapt to the realisation that the violence itself has changed him; his aim has become impossible because it is his character and outlook as it was before the violence he has committed that he cannot now restore. Every one of the better suspense writers, so much without exception that this could well be

121

the one common factor that separates them from the rest, seems to have some interest in and understanding of this aspect of characterisation.

There might be other workable tests for subtlety, but for any kind of complicated narrative the only test known to me that answers most of the time is that change must be *incremental* rather a sudden reversal. The interesting point to a writer about the events on the road to Damascus is not the revelation in the light but the character's conditioning beforehand that leads him to be persuaded by it. (The same sort of burning-bush material is much better handled elsewhere in the Bible.) Only in inspirational texts does such revelation work *because* it is God's word, deus ex machina; everyone but the faithful wants to know what went before, or as one film editor is wont to say, 'Where's your build-up to the bush, buddy?' There is a corollary question that is often useful: considering only the specifics of the narrative, and excluding literary conventions and expectations, can the character see the change coming before the reader can? He should be able to, being so closely involved. People do not have an experience and then change; instead their expectations interreact with the experience while it happens. Even a mugging occupies enough temporal space for the character to think of how he will pay the rent and to enjoy a flashing daydream of vengeance. (While a New York thug swung a chain at me, knocking chunks from the wall behind me, I wondered whether my mother would not have preferred a more dignified death for her number one son; I am also reliably told that under fire in the Congo I loudly recited Greek stanzas. Later I had the apparently brilliant idea of asking racing drivers what they had thought on the brink of death but had to give up the intention of turning their thoughts into Meaningful Literature because their concerns, when they were not too embarrassed to tell me, were no different from that of a man being prepped for an appendectomy and worrying about the unpaid bills except that the racing drivers' bills had a few more noughts on the end.) Dostoyevsky is excellent if you want to study this interrelationship of the character's motivations (lusts and other drives) with his actions (crimes), the whole interleaved with the price he knows he will have to pay.

There is also a sense in which certain subtleties seek you out or create themselves. It is good practice when you approach the end of a book to set aside some time to consider whether you have drawn together all the narrative strands. Obviously your main plot will be resolved, and your main subplots will not have escaped your attention either, but what about the sub-subplots? If you try to resolve everything as late as possible to enhance your final climax, these lesser resolutions have very limited space – and you might discover with pleasure that brevity in many cases inhabits the same space as subtlety. If they occur earlier in the book, these lesser climaxes and resolutions can often be made subtler merely by pruning their efflorescence in the cutting stages of your work.

Finally, there is a small trick that can sometimes save even the naturally melodramatic or otherwise awkward moment. This is symbolism, as in the Le Carré example above where the lighter symbolises the faithless wife – and more: the traitors who had been her lovers and his friends, on all of whom Smiley is now turning his back. A symbol is by nature a subtlety, and it almost always saves words as well, which makes it especially useful at the climax when the pace of the narrative will limit the physical space available. Symbols also get you kudos from the critics, who all fancy themselves iconographers of genius.

Of course, subtlety is relative to what went before and must be tailored for the intended audience. In *Roots of Violence*, Andrew McCoy allows his hero Lance Weber ('the quintessential hard man of Africa') to kill any number of slavers as he chases across Africa after his abducted wife Esmeralda. After having his characters storm an Arab princeling's island, liberate his harem, and install a new ruler, the author right on the last page of his book, after his main and secondary climaxes, draws in even the smallest strand by giving centre stage to a very minor character who, by comparison to what went before, is not only funny but actually subtle – and not likely to be forgotten:

Nasheer paused a moment to recollect her and in the

pause Lance said, 'Maria went with Harry Sabib.'

Maria took a jar from her basket and placed it on the edge of Nasheer's desk. 'Kidneys pickled in brine, Your Highness.' Next she put a small bowl on the desk. 'Liver, made into a pâté with a squeeze of gherkin juice.' Next a flat round plastic dish. 'Brawn. Your Highness may be quite certain I scraped it all quite clean, washed it repeatedly under running water, and cut out the ulcerated parts.'

'Christ, this I don't like,' Lance said.

But Maria seemed not to hear him. She put a small bottle on the desk. 'Eyes, roast, preserved in gelatine which should be melted away in slow heat before serving.'

Nasheer leaned forward to study the eyes. His own met Lance's and Lance said, 'I too have seen those eyes recently. And not on any sheep.'

But Maria merely smiled agreeably and produced another container. 'A patina of brains for spreading on toast, very good at breakfast.' Triumphantly she pulled the last dish from her basket. It was a saucer and covered by a small cloth. With a dramatic gesture she whipped the cloth away from two small round brown objects. 'And baked prairie oysters.'

Lance found Esmeralda standing beside him, as riveted by Maria's performance as he was.

'You are not well, Maria,' Nasheer said. 'But we have a doctor now and – '

'Tosh!' Esmeralda interrupted him. 'She's no more mentally disturbed than you or I. Look.' Esmeralda turned Maria around gently and raised her anklelength white dress to her middle. Maria wore nothing under the dress and she had long, tapering legs and handsome buttocks. Lance felt a stirring in his trousers. Then he saw the scars around her anus and in the small of her back and felt only pity.

'A man abused her,' Esmeralda said, letting the dress fall, 'so, when the opportunity arose, she killed him. Baking Harry Sabib's testicles in an oven is one version of woman's lib.'

'Arabia is the wrong place for woman's liberation, Esmeralda,' Lance said.

'All right, if she can't stay... Would you like to come with me to Kenya, Maria? I can always use an imaginative cook.'

Maria smiled and nodded enthusiastically.

'Just keep her away from my breakfast,' Lance muttered.

'What was that, dear? You're mumbling.'

'Oh, just that I'm partial to a bit of offal myself, as long as it is properly prepared.'

'Well, that's settled then. Come, Maria.' Esmeralda swept out with the murderess in tow.

Lance sat down and glared at Nasheer.

Nasheer said, 'Don't look at me. You're the one who's in trouble.'

BADDIES

Paradoxically those characters who are bad by design, evil, doers of dirty deeds, black hats, are easier to manage than the good guys who give the writer trouble (to whom we shall return). Perhaps this is because you can see them coming: you know the cause of their problem, and can brace yourself. The real black hats, baddies by nature or circumstance, seem to give even experienced writers trouble in direct proportion to the space he does *not* allocate for explaining their characters. That most narratives have a hero who by hogging the limelight severely limits the space available for the bad guys is an inescapable condition of by far the largest part of creative writing. The writer has to say more about the bad guys in less space – and that is the cause of most of his problems with them. We treat the symptoms, not the disease, because the disease cannot be cured without killing the patient: successful books that give the baddies equal time with the goodies are few and far between, and successful books that give the baddies equal *consideration* with the goodies can be counted and comprehensively discussed over dinner by any reasonably well read foursome.

A note of caution, if you don't mind. It would be easy to line up a dozen respected writers happy to pillory me for separating the treatment of characters in opposition to the protagonist from the mainstream remarks on characterisation. They may feel that all this talk of good guys and bad guys does not belong in a text for any but the crude sensationalist. But the language is intended for quick comprehension, not as an incitement for you to lower your standards, and the separation is essential because the *condition* of this class of character is different. Nor will the argument hold water that minor characters of perfect moral standing and exemplary behaviour suffer under the same spatial disability as the baddies: we know that the minor good guys enjoy in the reader's mind the benefit of doubt, gleefully withheld from the baddies. The upshot is that, even when the writer treats both classes the same in the writing, in the reading the baddies slip over the top into caricature, and worse, rather more easily than the good minor fellows. Whatever has been said elsewhere about dealing with the main good guys also applies to dealing with the black hats. But you can minimise the dangers imposed on the baddies by the accepted conventions of literature and the ingrained habits of readers if you apply your skills much more rigorously to the bad guys than to the good guys. In particular, the characterisation of bad guys must pass two additional key tests.

True villains are not permanent villeins No one is enslaved to evil. No one is born evil. No one does evil without a reason once they pass puberty. There is always a reason that the character understands and accepts. The impulse to evil for its own sake has little credence in psychology and none in literature. Only in melodrama is the villain bad *because* he is bad.

Even the possessed recognise a chain of cause and effect that makes sense to them at the time when they act or react. Talk to any psychologist who works with mentally disturbed persons, or any social worker or parole officer who deals with rapists, and you will soon grasp the only certainty such professionals can obtain from many of their clients: that contortions of reason are manifold. Interesting books remain to be written in this field but where deranged or disturbed people feature in books not primarily devoted to them, their precise reasoning is usually not as important as the reader's appreciation that it is warped.

All other classes of bad guys but the mentally disturbed should be motivated by logical, if not morally acceptable, chains of reasoning *acceptable to themselves* – including every point where the logic would, if submitted to an uncommitted arbitrator, fail an objective test. Readers much more readily view the doings of baddies objectively than those of sympathetic characters, so a black hat's twisted logic must be rigorously justified by the writer through the character.

You will probably by now have observed that this procedure meets several other tests, including those that rely on leaving no question unanswered, but the main importance of this test to the link between writer and reader is that in defining and quantifying the character's motivation (logic) with such rigour you are accepting it – not the same as condoning it – and therefore can present the character more convincingly.

The most basic drives of minor characters need no great superstructure of motivation: greed for thieves, lust for rapists, anger for murderers, desperation for drug addicts, and so on. The self-justification of the criminal, before and after the event, is often more interesting in its inventiveness than the unadorned, age-old and therefore boring original motive.

Motive may be used creatively. Truman Capote felt that it was infinitely more interesting to follow two characters who killed for kicks than low-level thugs who murder for money like all the other low class thugs. He was right. Furthermore, while anger at oppression or poverty seems, intellectually, a credible motivation for terrorists, those revolutionaries I have met have all been middle-class individuals who, in my opinion, were attracted to the gun more from boredom than conviction; psychologists who specialise in this work agree with my conclusions but novelists, on the whole, seem to find the protestations of the terrorists more convincing than the empirical work of the psychologists, and non-fiction writers often report without question what they are told by revolutionaries about their motivation and membership. It is precisely his understanding that the IRA terrorist is rooted in an intellectual (and distinctly unproletarian) tradition that makes the books of Jack Higgins on the subject refreshingly different and convincing while books fall flat whose authors accept the post-1968 public relations triumph of a marxist-proletarian revolt against an occupying imperial army.

Taking the easy target of racial bigotry, let us compare two films, *Cry Freedom!* directed by Richard Attenborough and *A Passage to India* directed by David Lean; choosing the films allows us to divorce them from the books on which they are based, one by a competent journalist, the other by a literary luminary. In *Cry Freedom!* to be black is to be good and to be white is to be bad; you can look up all the synonyms for good and bad in your thesaurus and add them here – the film misses no part of the catalogue. True, there is a token good white man, the hero, but all the rest of the whites are malevolent beyond belief and the direction makes clear whose intention this is. The film fails, lacking even the amusing malice of Mr Young's book on Mrs Thatcher; it also proves that in the absence of credible characters a glossy style and superb command of all the mechanical technicalities are wasted. In *A Passage to India* a warm surface and superior command of technique are similarly taken for granted but each character is wise or silly, compassionate or self-centred, brave or cowardly, and much more, according to his nature, regardless of the colour of his skin – and every character is complicated, without offensive oversimplifications. Because we believe in the characters we never question that this is what the experience of racism is really like.*

---

* Sir Richard is always earnestly eager to address 'the large issue' but his later films fail time and again to touch the true human chord. A Lean film by contrast seems told for the sake of telling a good story passionately well, and to address the universal issue almost by accident. We have been here before: it is the good story that matters – and the issue only if one can present it as touching on credible characters. It is probably not incidental that the best Lean films have screenplays by Robert Bolt, the greatest living British playwright.

Real evil   At an elevated level of this test there are evils so monstrous that we are tempted to draw the veil over them or, if that is impossible, to grow protective scar tissue on our intellect. Michiko Kakutani wrote in the *New York Times* of 5 December 1982 that: '...a kind of intellectual distancing has begun to occur in depictions of the Holocaust, which threatens to trivialize, even distort, the actual event.' In the introduction to his 1984 novel *The Angel of Zin* (Hodder & Stoughton) Clifford Irving expresses a heartfelt agreement with these remarks, and proposes a correct attitude for writers: 'It is the writer's obligation to make you see, feel, and ponder; the writer does not trivialise or distort historical events by shaping them into a design that is more visible, more deeply felt. It is not instructive to say, "Six million Jews were killed. Their Nazi murderers were beasts." Unless we are content to be victims of media simplism, it is necessary to know the names of some of those six million (even if those names are fictionalized), to see their faces, to empathise with their experience. It is also necessary to view the murderers not as beasts, but as men and women who abdicated their humanity in favour of warped visions, brute economic need and a dreadful conformity.'

With his theme and concept so clear in his own mind, it is no surprise that Mr Irving's novel succeeds. Len Deighton's novel *Winter* is another successful study of this particular abdication that proceeds from the same premise.

Gamesmanship   Does your baddie have a life outside the story? What does he do in his leisure time? Think of the drug dealers in bad books: they are one hundred per cent committed to their job. The planes, yachts and limousines are nothing more than adjuncts they use without enjoyment; the gourmet food is wolfed as fuel – I'm supplying the likely reasons, not quoting, because such books routinely don't supply any reasons. But the question immediately arises: if they do not enjoy the rewards, why do they bother to take such enormous risks? To use the money for keeping score in some game? Because they are addicted to the drug of danger? Pride in craftsmanship? Keeping up the family business? (A drugs baron in South America actually offered this reason: 'It is what my father did before me, and my sons will do after me.') Because they cannot stop for fear of their competitors killing them? Because they cannot stop for simple lack of will to change direction? Because they are anti-social? Because they are enemies of capitalism and wish to undermine it? One could continue for several pages. Any of these reasons are not only good, but suggest events that may extend and invigorate the characterisation and plot. The real reason why the drugs baron quoted above keeps up his business is that he maintains a private polo team of international standard – a four million dollar a year habit. Whatever the writer wants to work with – the character's expressed reason, or his real reason, or the contrast between them – is something for the reader to get his teeth into, to answer his questions. The writer who does not ask the questions and offer answers deserves and finds no readers.

Of course the handle does not need to be the private polo team of a drugs baron. It can be the stamp collection of a gentle master burglar or the love for his family of a crooked politician. It doesn't really matter what you choose as long as it gives the reader a perspective on the baddie that adds depth; what matters is that there be something credible besides malevolence.

Writers have a general down on television, and rightly because so much of it is bland, but the one teleseries many approve of is the early *Wiseguy*, starring Ken Wahl. This series portrays the life and work of an undercover agent of the Organised Crime Bureau of the FBI and is therefore based, at first sight, on the extremely shaky premise that the audience will hold sympathy with a protagonist whose whole life consists of winning the confidence of people only to betray them. It is an idea most producers will throw out before they blink on the ground that it is suffering from a terminal case of Duck's Disease. It is therefore just as well that the originator of the idea, the Canadian writer Stephen J. Cannell, is also the executive producer. 'Life and work' is not an idle phrase: the Cannell production team build sympathy by showing that the good guys have a life outside their work and that their work influences their families and friends and mental wellbeing. Many 'strictly commercial' television producers would cut this element, believing it to be 'beside the point of the main story'; or attempt to glamorise it. But Mr Cannell goes further: he turns the main disadvantage of his major premise, that his chief good guy must go on and on betraying people, into an advantage by showing these criminals as real people, great folks with families they love, some of them men and women who inspire loyalty and respect. Of course this magnifies the pain of having to turn them in, but the price is also what makes the characters credible. This already tramples on the received wisdom of what makes a long-running teleseries but Mr Cannell goes on to stomp: he doesn't only show his baddies as real people, he allows his heroes some doubt about who the baddies are! It is probably just as well this series is made in Toronto, a long way from the centres of tradition and convention in teleseries, or we might never have seen it. One would expect writers to approve, but so many of the general public chose it against the glossy *Miami Vice* when the two were recently available in concurrent time slots where I live, that the mere numbers must force one to conclude that people who never read a book are equally sensitive to the conventions of good literature. Or perhaps such viewers deduce from everyday experience that nothing and nobody is ever all black or all white and appreciate a writer, or television producer, who doesn't try to tell them apples are oranges. Certainly, if the couch potatoes know the difference, your readers will.

PROBLEMS, WARNINGS AND OPPORTUNITIES

There are two general classes of characters an author may have trouble with for reasons that are or should be under his control. Some of these problems are just that, problems to be solved, but others are warnings to the writer not to do something or to do it differently, and some may present opportunities to improve your book.

Out for a duck The smallest and most dangerous group

consists of characters a particular author discovers too late he should not write about because he lacks the background to handle them convincingly, except to the converted or the naive. This is a form of Duck's Disease and often proves fatal. The problem is made especially dangerous because the converted may include a publisher who will bring out the book because he agrees with the author's politics (and in fiction, political outlook) and then blame the writer when readers apply the stricter standards that the publisher should have applied but didn't. If you don't fancy reading Eisenhower biographies to monitor my example, try the fiction genre known as 'glitz' in which, if the author sets his sights low enough, research may be substituted for experience. For instance, Judith Krantz tells the reader the colour of the covers on the menus in all the best restaurants, something I cannot say I paid particular attention to either when I was in advertising and blessed with an unlimited expense account plus a professional interest in design and colour, or more recently when for seven or eight years I was associated with an agent and a publisher who were constitutionally incapable of conducting meaningful conversation anyplace other than expensive restaurants. The same superficiality carries over into the characters of such authors. The failures when these authors overreach themselves by depicting classes of people with whom they have only newspaper familiarity can make even the shallower bits from the novels of Robert Ludlum look like perceptive writing, simply because as a one-time film producer he did mix with the rich and the famous while the jumped-up pretenders have no experience beyond Brooklyn or Wilkes-Barre. Of course Ms Krantz and the rest may retort that their avid readers have even less experience of high life, and this may be a valid excuse at the lower, 'pure entertainment' end of the fiction market. Higher up the scale in fiction and always in non-fiction a greater truth is a precondition of quality and credibility which, as an additional difficulty for the writer, is always presumed to be judged by an informed reader. We have already touched on Duck's Disease several times and there is no more I know that can help you except this: have you considered dropping the

troubled book and starting another from scratch about characters you know? You can't go wrong with what you really
know rather than what you think you can find out.

Neutrality and other pacts   No one in his right mind will
argue that the writer should be or could be neutral to his
characters. It is however desirable for any convincing book
that the writer preserves a pretence of objectivity, and true
objectivity is a requirement of lasting art. But even true
objectivity has a special meaning in literature. It is the ability
of the author to hold fast to his own moral precepts while
presenting the character with the character's motivations
intact and imperative – what we mean when we say the
author draws the character 'from the inside'. We have
already mentioned the example of Ian Grey's biography of
Stalin which portrays the tyrant's outrages, from his own
viewpoint, as entirely reasonable; Joel Carmichael in *Stalin's
Masterpiece*, in which he argues that the show trials were
dramatic constructions with willing actors, performs the
same unlikely feat for the whole Russian intelligentsia. What
we are describing here is the author's ability to stand back
and withhold judgement until its proper place; in fiction the
judgement may appear to be withheld altogether though it is
in fact left to the reader, carefully and – the writer hopes –
invisibly guided to make the right judgement.

There is a simple test you may apply to all characters: ask
yourself if you are very much emotionally committed *against*
a character. Of course you cannot write very well about a
character unless he or she gives you some charge for or
against but it is a matter of acceptable degree.

If you love a character too much you may be blinded to his
faults and he will come off your page like St Francis of Assisi.
This is not necessarily a disaster if you're into inspirational
literature but it is much less acceptable in almost all other
branches of creative writing because it conflicts with the
requirement for objective truth.

With characters you don't like you have much less lati-
tude. In fiction they may simply turn out to be best-quality
plywood, which is bad enough if they are leading characters,

but in non-fiction they are extremely dangerous because your dislike may blind you to their motivation and your book, despite your best intentions, will fail. (We are not discussing the condemnatory tract, which is by intention and execution dishonourable; we will assume that your intentions are towards decent objectivity, supported by a belief in the intelligence and good judgement of your readers.) You may not admire my solution to this problem – which is never to write about characters I dislike so intensely that I reject out of hand all their reasons for all their actions – but it does keep me out of trouble; there seems to me to be a substantial difference between proving one's courage and accepting a suicide mission. This is a matter of perspective and the ability to compartmentalise your mind, brought home to me when I asked a friend how, as a Jew, he could pretend to write objectively about Hitler. 'But I'm not writing as a Jew. I'm writing as an economist interested in inflation. Genocide is a separate matter. Do you approve of Zaharoff the pedlar of arms and fomenter of wars?' No, I don't. In fact, what attracted me to the episode in Zaharoff's life around which I built a novel that took four years out my life was precisely the opposite, that in a largely reprehensible life his wartime mission to Germany was the one incontrovertibly altruistic act. Were there not already a definitive biography by Donald McCormick, I would consider that small empathy an adequate reason for concluding that I did not see the man entirely black and could therefore contemplate writing a biography about him myself. The question is not one of objective evil but rather: did the character in your opinion ever do anything right – and that one thing for what you consider the right reasons? If your opinion of a politician is that he was a stumblebum who did the right thing only by accident or because he was skiving off on the golf course while his aides took the decisions, that doesn't qualify. If there's absolutely nothing on which you can find common ground with a character *on his terms and for his reasons*, stand clear, unless what you truly want is to do a hatchet-job. However, *in his terms* your bond with the character need not be large or important; *to you* its importance is the thread it gives you by which you can unravel the rest of his character. In practice your empathetic connection with a bad man is likely to be only a small part of his personality or actions. But it is your guarantee that you will not create a character with the consistency of toffee, and a touchstone for most of the requirements for living, lasting characters we discussed above.

It is not necessary for the subject of the bond to be generally considered positive. If your subject is W. C. Fields, it would help if you were a witty sourpuss: 'No man can be all bad who hates children and dogs.'

Difficult minor characters   If a character gives you trouble in creating him it is useful to evaluate his importance to the story. If he is a very minor character, can you do without him? Is it really worth investing a disproportionate amount of time in understanding him to the extent that he no longer troubles you? In fiction this is an easy decision – slash and on to the next. In non-fiction it often pays to look at the character's influence on events and other characters: is his impact duplicated elsewhere? If so, out. This is a plotting error and has nothing to do with characterisation; the character is troublesome to signal his desire to depart.

If the obstructive character in your present conception is spatially minor but motivationally essential, this is often a clue that you are not allowing him the space he needs to establish himself, in short that you have underestimated his importance. It is not easy to be precise here but my own experience has always been that the character in this condition has been too closely pruned and that reference to my notes shows what should be put back in; it must be theoretically possible that the writer does not know enough about the character, in which case more research or thought should answer, but in all except the most unusual instances a lack of knowledge would be obvious from a failure of the chain of motivation at an early planning stage rather than when you are already writing your book.

There is an even rarer case of a troublesome minor character. An editor reports that one of his writers early in her career wasted a week trying to build up a character on whose action the whole book pivoted but who was otherwise of no account: 'The ambassador travelling incognito was recognised by the conductor of the train, with unfortunate consequences. It was a waste of the writer's time to try and build up the conductor's character to substantiate the coincidence. In fact, this is one of those instances where the coincidental, random nature of an event is its strength. The book read better when the conductor was not named or in any way particularised.' Quite so. But in my heart I sympathise with the writer rather than with her editor; coincidence has so little place in decent writing that an author might be excused for not recognising it when he stumbles over it, and distrusts it intensely when it is warmly introduced to him by an editor who until now has denied its very existence. (Is there any writer who has not been rapped by an editor for coincidence, for lack of motivation or, more pretentiously, for including a deus ex machina?) The old saw about not naming minor characters is too much hedged about with qualification and exception to be of much use, and here would have been a red herring anyway because 'minor' is always understood to refer to influence on events rather than the space occupied by a character. However, if in your own work you meet this case of a minor character wielding a disproportionate influence through some comparatively minor act, instead of trying to build him up you may like to try the alternative of emphasising his insignificance by telling us nothing more about him than his function and what he did. Thriller writers and historians alike are familiar with an offstage prime minister or president almost offhandedly setting in motion a chain of events that will significantly change the lives of others; it might on this analogy be quite impactful to bring them briefly and impersonally on stage to do their bit.

Major league pains   All the above applies to minor characters only. Major characters should not give a writer with even a little experience trouble in the writing except in some very specific circumstances; some we have already met under other headings and a few we shall discuss now. No pretence is made at a comprehensive list; such a thing would be impossible. But don't forget the tenor of this whole book, its premise, that for the good things in writing you look to your characters. Conversely, when you have gone wrong, check first whether the fault lies in characterisation. In ninety-nine cases out of every hundred you will have to look no further.

Leading characters who refuse to shine   Assuming that the character's chain of motivation appears complete, it must then follow that he is dull on the page because there is something about him you have misinterpreted. Quite often one comes across cases where experienced writers know that the dull drag of writing a character is a warning but cannot quite fathom what is wrong. First, always ask whether you are not forcing some moral viewpoint of your own on the character. I made a point of seeking an introduction to one of the writers whose work on Eisenhower just didn't taste right in the mouth. If this writer were ever asked to run for president, he would immediately say yes, not because of immodesty but because a sense of duty and a love of politics run in his family. He could not understand that Eisenhower demurred a) because it was no part of a military man's duty to run for the office, b) until it was made clear to him it was his duty as a citizen to save the republic (I'm not joking: that was precisely the view Harry Luce of *Time* privately conveyed to the general again and again), and c) because his background and upbringing frowned on too naked an ambition and expected polite modesty. That writer's conclusion that Eisenhower was a hypocrite follows logically from applying his own moral precepts to Eisenhower's actions. It is inconceivable to him that in such a serious matter there could be more than one proper way to act.

Lytton Strachey, a gleefully unreliable witness, is a better read on the Victorians than many a more sober scholar because at least he understood their motivations – how else could he have ridiculed them so effectively? – whereas the modern scholar judges them by his own values and so misleads the writer doing his research. Frankly, I have given up hope of ever grasping the essence of the Victorians;

Bismark's Prussians are much easier for an economist to understand, and as an epicure I understand the Edwardians better than their forebears; of course it means I cannot write about the Victorians.

This problem may be easier to grasp with a more recent illustration. Imagine you are eavesdropping on two middle-aged publishers beside the bar. One says, 'I spent the sixties getting laid.' The other says, 'I spent the sixties making my first million.' Neither of them can remember much about the issues that so inflamed and separated them at the time. We're near enough to them to write about either according to our views on the permissive society or the resurgence of capitalism, or we can make a point by accepting both views as different sides of the same coin. Undoubtedly such men had their equivalents in Victorian society: the problem arises when you try to transfer your assessment of their differences onto, say, Sir Richard Burton's trouble with the establishment over his translation of the *Arabian Nights*. Nobody seems to be able to make clear why his widow felt she had to burn his papers and we are left to conclude that she was a bigot, which is inconsistent with what else we know of her. (I am familiar with this example because Burton is a surefire hero for my kind of novel; him I understand perfectly but I cannot write about him because the true reasons for his contemporaries' reaction to him are a closed book.)

It is not only politics, time and background that divide. Sex divides; examples abound on any library shelf. Money is said to divide – my experience is that it does not, at least not in the levelled-off Western society or at the top of the others where the gulf between the aristocrats, the very rich, and the professional classes is often more spoken about than actual. What divides is education and privilege, nowhere more so than in Russia before Gorbachev. In the very poorest parts of Africa caste – tribal affiliation and patronage connections – divides as much as in India and, as in India, counts for more than mere possession of money. But *attitudes* to money do influence the judgements writers make about their characters. Some rightwing historians classify characters according to their attitude to their own money and everyone else's. Ayn

Rand's novel *Atlas Shrugged* can be conveniently analysed by this mechanism. But in this case a declared bias (Miss Rand founded a philosophy of self-sufficiency called Objectivism) is merely the author's admission of sharing her character's motivation, which is the same as saying the writer understands it perfectly. The terrifying thing about this novel is that Miss Rand, presumably as the result of her experience of being dispossessed in Russia by the Bolsheviks, understands the motives of those characters who do not carry her approval with an insidious impartiality which enables her to make weakness seem a crime – a conclusion that in our softer, more forgiving age makes many critics uncomfortable. But the historians are on the side of Miss Rand: the most inhuman crimes are committed because the weak do not resist. Whether you agree with her politics or not, for any writer interested in technique Miss Rand's masterpiece must be James, the brother of the heroine; he is a whining, self-pitying rich slob of the kind any self-respecting human being wants to kick in the face. I choose this unpopular example (unpopular with critics, that is – this book has been a best seller for over forty years) because so positive a person as Miss Rand must have worked very hard to get inside a character whose every breath is repugnant to her. James is precisely everything she is not; that makes him the ideal example to other writers of a character presented on his own terms and left to the judgement of the reader.

Your character's unique perspective on events   If a character seems wishy-washy, undirected, the sort of fellow you cannot get a handle on, don't mistake this for dullness and panic because you fear you are incapable of understanding something crucial about his motivation. As always, check that the chain of motivation is closed, but if it is ask yourself another question: What is this character's unique perspective on these events? If he sees them precisely as every other character does, he will have no friction with them – the cause of the apparent dullness – and be superfluous.

Andrew McCoy wrote on this subject: 'Regardless of how perfect agreement is in any group on the desired objective or the means to reach it, many, many decisions have to be taken during action to achieve the objective, which is bound to throw up different opinions on how to proceed. Furthermore, any plan proceeding against opposition – a common literary occurrence – is likely to require initiative and improvisation, another source of friction. Stories about the armed services have an archetypal quality. A platoon of soldiers is trained under physical and emotional stress to suppress individual traits so that they may act as one. In a battle, under even greater physical and emotional pressure, their individual characters will again be revealed.' This implies that each character already has a unique outlook which colours his reaction to events as soon as the 'pressure' is great enough. Conversely it implies that any essential character who lacks his own outlook was created for the event, which is a prime no-no – manipulation when what you need is motivation.

If you cannot do without a character until he is required in a key scene, and if you cannot cut his part in earlier sections almost to insignificance, you must *discover* that he has a unique viewpoint on events so that he may be placed in friction with one or more of the other characters to add to the tension and pace of the story.

An obstreperous drunk is a character with a unique viewpoint – everyone is his enemy – and instant friction, but the type of character we are discussing must have a reason to get drunk (unless he is an alcoholic, in which case he already has a unique viewpoint and wouldn't be troubling us under this head). My all-purpose question, 'What does this character fear most?' often works; logically another good question must be, 'What does this character want most?' If you have a bunch of people on a sports squad, they all want to win: but one wants fame, another money, one to impress women, another to prove his courage, another plays because his best friend is on the team, yet another because it is an opportunity to develop leadership talents, and one so that his father can live vicariously through him.

The unpleasant character   There are some characters whose

140

faces you want to grind under your heel even as you write them. This is normally a good sign. As you have no doubt concluded by now, while we may believe in the sincerity of any writer who claims he's truly neutral to his characters, we must inevitably find such a writer's wisdom flawed. Most books have bad guys and anyone with a decent moral centre – which surely describes most authors – dislikes bad people even as he makes his ritual bow towards compassion and understanding. What's the point of expending a lot of hard work delineating a bad guy if your readers don't get the message that they should dislike or hate him (or, at the highest levels of literature, pity him); note that we are discussing a narrative requirement of friction and tension that has nothing to do with any moral duty politically inspired critics try to impose on writers.

In Nelson De Mille's novel *The Charm School* he depicts an extremely unpleasant character called Colonel Burov, an unreconstructed Stalinist in a glasnost age. The danger with such characters is always that one can send them up so easily, the reader somehow getting the idea that the writer is nudging him, saying, *Just between us civilised people, nobody can really be that bad because it would undermine our liberal faith in the essential goodness of Man.* However, Burov believes in terror not because he is a sadist but because he has seen it work. Mr De Mille creates an opportunity for Burov to say outright that he terrorises his subordinates and his own bosses terrorise him – because terror works. It is a key scene in the book, helping the reader understand the Russian psyche. Mr De Mille is far too smart a writer to make overt ex cathedra judgments but his reader cannot escape the correct conclusion – unless he is a Russian reader of a certain reactionary frame of mind, in which case he might consider Burov the tragic hero of the story! That's a good test, that readers who do not agree with your hero should at the very least feel that his opponents are worthy of carrying their banner into battle; better still, the motivation of the bad guys should be presented so sympathetically that readers who share their views might conclude that the author does too.

So far we have talked about a character that is designed to be a bad guy. But what if your hero is an unpleasant character, necessarily so in non-fiction because you have to work with what is historically true, by choice in fiction because that is what you desire for some narrative reason? Unless you are making a point of some kind, usually political, I suggest you'd better not start on a book whose chief character you dislike. A hatchet job might give you some malicious glee but a book whose characters give you no pleasure at all will be dull to write and to read. Furthermore, it makes sense to keep negative, rather than unpleasant, characters as small as possible. Negative characters presented realistically are depressing to write and can be tiresome to read; a big negative character can also, though I don't know how or why, impose a downbeat spiral on all the rest of your writing. If a character is a drag, he usually makes much more of an impression on the reader in a small space than a more positive character. The ineffectual, self-pitying housewife caught up in a natural disaster needs only a couple of pages to impress her indelibly on the mind of readers, whereas her sister the self-starting schoolteacher needs quite a few pages – but at least they're more fun to write.

Anti-heroes   In any kind of story where Johnny Average is dumped in unusual circumstances and has to adapt, he is technically an anti-hero. This maverick definition can be helpful to writers if they keep an open mind. In the Eisenhower example cited, the writers who failed all looked through the wrong end of the telescope, seeing a world-conqueror and international statesman who inexplicably refused to behave as they thought a conqueror and statesman should; the writers who succeeded looked into the other end of the telescope and asked how this smalltown boy became the most successful soldier in the history of the world, not to mention a particularly effective President, and why. It is useful to look into the origins and history of your character *from his viewpoint at that time* even if your story starts much later. An aged English earl once told me that any real aristocrat by the age of five can swear like a stablehand; he was discussing a love of horses, but think what other attitudes are formed in a child who spends his time in the stables, to bloodlines and breeding for instance, to the very lives of those too old to serve, and so on.

There is another sense in which 'anti-hero' is commonly used: to describe a man who is less well equipped than he should be for the circumstances given him by his creator, as if a Woody Allen persona were dropped into a James Bond job. This is tricky to handle well to such an extent that one wonders whether some very successful comedies in this style were intentional or happened because their creators, aiming for something loftier, failed to control the method. But when successful, the anti-hero can be the basis for a lasting book. Eric Ambler's protagonists are commonly anti-heroes and it is instructive to reread his early books and analyse how he turns the weak and self-pitying into such sly survivors. This is not to advise that you try to emulate him in any particular. However, Mr Ambler's work and the other successful non-humorous examples hold a lesson: that the writers who do anti-heroes well have a bent for irony, either on a darkly heroic and universal scale, like Dostoyevsky, or on a personal, bazaar-cubicle scale, like Mr Ambler. (I imply no value judgement between classes of irony, merely different approaches to the same conclusion.)

Finally, there is a class of writing that is also said to have anti-heroes but should rather be termed anti-heroic. Where the intention is to depict 'today's little people' going about their daily business, the writer is engaged in an exercise in futility; literature is by definition about the exceptional, the novel, the interesting. The little people have plenty of voice and voices, ranging from democratic votes for populist politicians to the cultural thugs of the yellow press who pander to their prejudices; they require no assistance from art. However, there are two exceptions to this rule. One deals not with the living 'little people' but with the dead 'common man': historians can reconstruct a most interesting picture of what life was like in a different age by following in minute detail the everyday activities of John and Jane Medieval. The fascination here is precisely the discomfort and unremitting toil of those distant lives, the ever-present danger from a hooligan state, and the other dramatic differences between their lives and ours; in its own way this facination conforms to the rule that literature is about the novel and consequently interesting aspects of the lives of others. It is therefore not an exception to the rule that kitchen sink literature fails but its proof from beyond the grave. The other exception comes from the work of anthropologists describing the daily lives of people, usually primitive, separated from us by distance or sophistication; the life of a woman who while washing her dishes in the river could lose an arm to a crocodile is fascinating for obvious reasons.

How to know you're over the top   The best early warning system against going over the top is to have a sense of humour. If on rereading your material you laugh aloud at the death scene, you're over the top. A young biographer says that while writing about a business meeting to plan an Anglo-German gas pipeline, she several times thought, And take that, you filthy Hun! Sure enough, rereading her work later made her wonder if she had turned into John Buchan. She was bored with the characters and went too far to inject interest. Further discussion revealed that she was ignorant of the wider implications of the meeting, and not really interested in the commercial reasons behind the desert adventures of her hero. Ignorance and boredom pushed her characters over the top. At least she was saved by her sense of humour.*

Furthermore, the writer with a sense of humour will allow his characters to express their own humour – and the leavening of humour in a character is almost always a guarantee that he is not over the top. This is especially true of people who can laugh at themselves, who by definition cannot take

---

* She had two choices: she either had to make an effort to understand what the meeting was about or restructure her story to move the meeting offstage. The solution in cases like this must be tailored to your intended audience. If you are writing a scholarly book, you must go the distance to understand and clarify even what does not truly interest you; conviction is less important than covering your back comprehensively. But my young friend was writing for popular consumption and here the assumption must be that what most interests the writer will carry the greatest conviction and therefore most interest the general reader, and conversely that what bores the writer will also bore the general reader.

themselves too seriously.

If you have a sense of humour but have simply never thought of it in relation to your own work, perhaps you should consider that all of us see or hear or experience something amusing every day, so why shouldn't characters in books? I'm not talking about one-liner wit, which can in its own place be useful, but of the humour inherent in situations; obviously small ironies are more prevalent than side-splitting set pieces. It is a commonplace among writers who have ever been in personal danger that stress brings out unexpected wit in the driest of people. Even gallows humour draws its credibility more from the analogy of experience than from incongruous contrast. There is opportunity for quietly unobtrusive wit in the telling of your story, in the apt words and phrases you choose.

The danger for those without a sense of humour is that they take themselves and their creations so seriously that when they go wrong it is easy for them either not to notice or, when the fault is pointed out to them, to blame the character rather than look to their understanding of the character. It may be that there are stories too serious to contain the slightest humour but I have never come across them; they are probably not acted out by humans. T. W. Adorno's remark that after the Holocaust it is impossible to write poetry must be metaphorical and rhetorical because otherwise it would display an ignorance of human nature no one would wish to saddle any poet with, least of all a good one. Thomas Keneally's *Schindler's Ark*, dealing directly with the Holocaust by presenting as fiction the true story of a German who saved many Jews from the gas chamber, is so successful, so appealing, precisely because it is a hugely good-humoured book; were the style unrelievedly grim to match the material, the book would have been just another breast-beating exercise in global guilt and would have deserved to fail. It can almost be said that Mr Keneally sneaks his message in by the back door: you're well into the story before you notice this is another Holocaust novel, and by then you are too well hooked to leave off.

A sense of humour is impossible to cultivate in those born

without it. Fortunately most writers have it, or at least possess very substantial wit, a more refined, literary form of humour that may pass for the real thing if the wit is not too astringent. If you somehow became a writer because, say, your sense of style was mistaken for wit, you should either confine yourself to those genres where style alone may carry you (coffee table books, political hatchet jobs, belles lettres, social bitchery, books created for the premier literary prizes)* or pay very special attention to objectivity in presenting characters and to fairness between your characters because you will have no other guarantee that you are presenting people and not gargoyles. Writers without the benefit of humour who stick very closely to what they know intimately – which is hard for the writer who must keep up enough momentum to earn a living – need never suffer the disadvantages of their lack. One of the most moving pieces I have ever read was a tribute to his mother by the most relentlessly unsmiling writer it was ever my misfortune to meet in person, but his lifetime output was less than the average pro publishes every thirty months.

Points of view   There is a wretched class of handbook for aspiring writers written by people who should have stuck to academia: they are characterised by offering as a planning device the point of view from which the story is told. This is stupid because the writer who tells his story through his characters instinctively knows which literary device is best for telling each character's story.

Please do not construe anything in this section as either advice that you should consciously consider points of view

---

* There could also be a career waiting for you in American publishing, where editors positively hate humour unless it is so well integrated as to be almost invisible, leaving only a generally good-humoured tone to illuminate the narrative. In some genres overt humour is unacceptable to most editors on either side of the Atlantic. Science fiction is one such, though these editors seem to have missed the point that any What If? literature depends for its success on the global, even universal, irony of comparing a possible future with the present reality. I can name at least three editors who would strike the deflating allusion to pompous scifi predilections ('global, even universal') from the previous sentence, and insist on writing 'science fiction' full out in this one. That doesn't mean they are right and I am wrong: the same fellows, and all their co-believers in the humourlessness of readers, have never noticed that the work of Kurt Vonnegut or Isaac Asimov is profoundly funny. They are so poorly or so narrowly educated and read, and so little capable of thinking for themselves, that they cannot conceive that profundity may coexist in the same space as amusement.

until they force themselves upon you or, most particularly, as incitement to vary points of view merely to show you are aware of them. (Bernard Levin observed of E. L. Doctorow's novel *Ragtime* that the author's insistence on varying writing formats as if presenting a literary kaleidoscope is authorial exhibitionism that interferes with the reader's grasp of the story. I cannot think of an example where points of view are varied merely as authorial exhibitionism; perhaps such books are so obviously bad that none reach publication.)

The most common viewpoint is the god's-eye view, known in classrooms as the third person impersonal. This technical term describes a book where the author tells the story as observed from above, seeing all the characters and all their motivations as if they were a glassed colony of ants with viewing ports inset into their brains. The term is misleading both as to the intent of literature and the reality of creating it. As we have seen, there is nothing impersonal about the author: he has an opinion about and an attitude to each of the characters, though he tries to hide it. As for the third person, it must be a dull reader who cannot tell you something of the unseen, unmet author after reading his book. The author who puts nothing of his personality into his book must be even duller, or command such superhuman powers of articulation – which is not the same as expression – that his humanity must be in doubt. That is why I prefer the less formal name of god's-eye view for this narrative method.

Normally the god's-eye view comes to most writers without alternatives being considered. We tell what each character did in turn – 'A did this. Then B did that.' – and the reader knows where our sympathies lie from the internal evidence of whom we pay the most attention to. It is probably the best way to tell the vast majority of stories, if simply because any other method has its own set of usually worse problems and may cause chopping and changing between viewpoints or characters that will only confuse the reader. The few stories that require a different narrative technique will usually announce themselves quite early in the planning stage; it is not uncommon among the writers I know for the narrative technique and subject to come into their minds together: 'Well, I know my other books are all third person impersonal but it never occurred to me this one should be anything but first person. I never thought about it until you mentioned it just now.'

The alternative to the god's-eye view is almost always to tell the story in the first person, directly from the viewpoint of one of the characters: 'I was born under a wandering star.' The character telling the story is usually the main character but need not be; a king's jester is in a position to observe almost everything the king experiences. Below we shall return to the special problems that first person narratives create for the writer.

A fairly uncommon combination of the two main viewpoints is the single person impersonal, in which the author tells the reader nothing that is not in a single character's immediate ken, that does not happen to him or near him or is not said within his hearing, but distances the narrator from the character by designating him 'he' rather than 'I'; Andrew Garve used this format to great effect in *A Hero for Leanda* .

There are a few more alternatives to or variations on the two main viewpoints but they too normally announce themselves. The evidence of the love between Michael Collins, the Irish revolutionary hero, and Kitty Kiernan is their letters: it must have been a natural decision for the compiler of *In Great Haste* to let them tell their own story through selected letters. Similarly, where extensive diaries exist one can usually let the diarists speak for themselves to much greater effect than by paraphrase.

Most of these formal considerations are irrelevant to the writer whose narrative method has come to him as a package with his story. However, sooner or later in the writing he will stumble across an opportunity to improve his book by switching points of view – and in most instances not recognise it, because nothing in his formal education prepared him for it. But the writer practising the god's-eye view does already switch viewpoints – every time he switches to the actions of another character. From there it is only a small step to telling parts of the story in the first person or a more esoteric format.

Mixing and matching   How do you know the time has arrived to switch viewpoints? If you're switching between characters in the god's-eye view, the narrative itself announces the point: it is time for the next event in the chain of motivation. That's simple and seems natural after a little practice – only novices extend a scene that has served its purpose. Apart from this routine, the opportunity for change is announced by problems, most often those that arise as a result of imposing values on a character from without rather than applying his convictions from within. The biggest difficulty which may be cured by a switch to a different viewpoint is that of the character you cannot get a handle on with the other methods described in this chapter. Try writing such a character in the first person; you might suddenly understand him better. If he is the leading character, let him tell his tale in the first person for the whole book. If he is a large character other than the leading character, and especially if you are also having problems with the leading character, your difficulty could be a tip that he should be the leading character instead.

Books with a first person hero seem to me to work better if the viewpoints are not mixed.

The downside of 'I'   Using the first person narrative is so often fraught with danger that you should trust only those guides who are well versed in the practice of what they preach. Unfortunately such guides divide very neatly into two fundamentally opposed camps. One group of gurus tells novices to stay clear of first person narratives; the other group feels that the first person is by far the most natural way to tell a story, including the first novel – which is generally agreed to be the most difficult literary barrier to surmount. I belong to the first group, because I have seen the first person cause new writers too much frustration and failure; but readers of this book are all a good deal further along in experience and perhaps in literary maturity. To enable you to make an informed decision, I list a few difficulties with first person narratives even experienced writers may encounter.

It is theoretically possible to have every character in the

book tell his story in the first person but modern examples of continuous booklength narrative – as opposed to discrete tales – done in this manner are few and far between. It is simply too confusing for the modern reader who has much less time to consider and digest each book than his counterpart a century ago; he doesn't have the time, the inclination, or the experience to pick his way through complicated structures.

A character that you understand better in the first person but cannot present directly in the first person because that will confuse your reader can be allowed to express himself through telling his story to an audience, writing letters, writing diaries, being put on a witness stand or otherwise giving evidence, and so on. This always brings ancillary complications; sometimes the contortions of writers trying to extricate themselves from these viewpoint mazes are of intrinsic interest.

In my novel *Reverse Negative* the main story was told by an elderly don in his diary, obviously entirely from his viewpoint. This left me with two problems: there was no sympathy left for the other characters; and I had no way of telling their story straightforwardly because my main character could not be present at all their events and could not know what was in their hearts. Furthermore, I wanted to present the antagonists as sincere men, and that was impossible to do in my main character's diary unless I made him saintly and forbearing beyond belief: these men were sincerely attempting to kill not only him but his cat.* After a great deal of experimentation and writing over forty drafts I hit on the expedient of presenting the main character's story through his diary, with the actions of all other characters inserted as computer-generated probability studies of what they were likely to have done in the given circumstances. This

---

* The last half of this sentence is loaded with the kind of humour one American critic describes as 'involuntary' and that is hated by American editors working at the commercial end of the market. In a novel intended for publication in New York, I would at the very least cut the word 'sincerely' and remove reference to the cat either altogether or into a separate, dully declaratory sentence. 'Saintly and forbearing beyond belief' is probably suspect too, even without the incongruous balance of the cat.

allowed everyone, including the black hats, to act as if they were steeped in good faith; it also added the small bonus of statistical uncertainty, which increased the tension of the story (what if the computer was wrong and on its evidence the hero accused an innocent?); and it actively made a point I was keen on about modern intelligence work being largely the stamping ground of business school graduates and computer programmers rather than trigger men.

First person black hats   It is possible to tell the story in the first person from the villain's perspective but not advisable except to the sublimely confident author – an entirely mythical creature – because the special difficulties of the format so greatly outweigh any possible advantage. I shall cite just two of the main problems. First, bringing your baddie to the realisation of his moral degeneracy is difficult enough, but what do you do when the crime merits the ultimate punishment? It always seems a cop-out when the author leads Rico to the electric chair and drops the curtain just as Rico sees the lever pulled; even worse is having to cut away at the climax to a secondary character to witness Rico's punishment. Even with lesser bad ends, say a cruel character being ostracised, we normally deduce the degree of the baddie's punishment from the reaction of sympathetic characters with whom we identify. Second, in any kind of writing that has a large measure of suspense, telling the baddie's story in the first person yet not revealing the key until the end implies that you cannot show any part of his mental process. The convention is that if you show any part of a character's mental process, readers expect you to show all, which would wreck suspense in a first person narrative by a baddie. If you show only part of his mental process but withhold the crucial part from readers until it suits you, they will rightly feel cheated. If you don't believe me, read Noel Hynd's otherwise excellent *False Flags*, where Mr Hynd shows only part of the baddie's mind until the very end of the book, and there cruelly disappoints his reader's faith in the author's honesty. This sort of error is virtually unavoidable with first person narratives of baddies. The solution, telling the reader only what the character says and does but not his thought processes beyond superficial observation of events and characters, is only for experts – try Len Deighton for examples, and note that even he does not try for first person black hats.

Dialogue, description, action   You know already that character should be revealed in action rather than merely on your say-so in flat, dead authorial statement. You may have noticed from your reading that commercially successful books avoid lengthy, passive descriptions of places. Leaving aside books created for the literary prizes, which are thin so that the publisher does not lose too much in printing costs when the book does not win the prize and is consequently unsaleable, most books from established writers are these days thicker than only a decade ago, the more so the nearer one approaches to the big-money commercial end of the market. There seems a contradiction here, but it is only apparent: most of the writers I read seem to use the extra space not so much to extend the action as to increase their depth of characterisation. It is often said that the necessity for quick and accurate characterisation inside the prefered length of 60–70,000 words which still applies to hardback detective fiction is what makes it such an excellent training ground for writers; but that is a good reason for beginners to write a detective novel, not a sound reason to limit everyone to that length. Even when publishers desire longer books it may be as well not to become too dependent on the luxury of so much space, because the pendulum always swings back and in hard times the first decision many publishers take is to prefer novels no longer than the magic 100,000 words.

'Action' is writers' shorthand for the active voice rather than the passive, as well as active representation instead of passive description. Dialogue is action, and so is thought, and so is observation by a character: for the author to describe a range of hills is description but for a character to view the hills through binoculars is action. Many readers must cringe, perhaps without quite knowing why, when incompetent or careless authors pass up such obvious opportunities to communicate more effectively. If one of your characters is present in a scene, there is always a way of putting the experience into the character's perspective rather than the author's – and you should do it. There are of course examples where no character is present – the best known being J. B. Priestley's description of Bradford and Dylan Thomas's Milk Wood – but they are by definition exceptions, are normally of an introductory nature, are commonly quite short, usually imply that the town or geographic feature being described is a character in the story, and as soon as possible turn to describing people. One good reason for preferring action and the active voice is that it helps the writer avoid many of those problems which arise from not understanding his characters perfectly; the other important reason is that it enhances communication with readers to address them through the characters with whom they identify. Furthermore, passive description that enhances tension is almost a contradiction in terms, with in all literature perhaps a handful of successful examples. On the other hand, surroundings seen through a character's emotional filter carry their own precisely measured tension.

Action and the active voice offer the writer great benefits at almost no cost and for very little additional effort. Don't miss out!

In this chapter we have delved into the mechanisms by which proper characterisation forwards both the writer's story and his communication with readers. The chapter is not comprehensive because it can never be: the purpose is rather to illuminate the daily detail of an attitude of mind. The profitable attitude is that character is central to literature: without a character who acts and reacts the writer has no story and therefore cannot write. In the immortal words of playwright Tom Stoppard: 'There is a problem with writing. It is writing the next line. Usually that is determined by the line before.'

6
MINING GOLD
FROM VERBIAGE
CUTTING AND REWRITING

IT is no accident that so many of the great film directors started their careers as film editors. A film editor is a man with a razor blade who cuts out all scenes and frames that do not directly contribute towards telling the story; superfluous shots (events) are thrown on the floor. It is an apprenticeship aimed in the first instance at a thorough understanding and appreciation of narrative structure. This is a skill writers must teach themselves at their typewriters or – as a distant second best – from a book like this.

Around the time my second book was published I thought that when I became a professional author I would be free of all that hateful cutting and rewriting. This was a risible misunderstanding and wishful thinking of the most naive kind. A professional writer is almost defined by the fact that he cuts and rewrites and cuts and rewrites and again and again, until he gets it right. Perhaps there are other experienced writers out there who still have not lost all hope of some day learning to get it right the first time every time, in which case perhaps we should start an Optimists' Club; but in our hearts we all know that any extended piece of writing which achieves perfection in the first draft is a very rare event. A striving towards perfection is the hallmark of every professional, not just writers. But whereas other professionals understand that a time limit is set by an hourly rate, the best writers (like the best artists in every field) have a compulsion to perfection that recognises no barrier. It is, I think, a compulsion a writer should cultivate and accept as a

154

natural part of his profession and his being. Such confirmation is an important step towards viewing cutting and rewriting as positive work, not an undesirable necessity like filing. Once you believe in cutting and rewriting as a positive contribution not only to your finished work but to the satisfaction of your urge to perfection, it follows that soon you will discover ways of making your cutting and rewriting more efficient.

A writer's tools   You should work with whatever tools you feel at home with. Most professional writers seem to buy the best of whatever writing tools they prefer, be it a fountain pen or a computer.

We have no space to go into the pros and cons of the electrified writer but don't let the prejudice of middle-aged Luddites put you off the computer. Maybe they love retyping; perhaps they are so insensitive that they never notice their secretary's face when a page has to be retyped for the umpteenth time; or could it be that they are resigned to sending out a less than perfect text? The advantage of the computer word-processor is that it allows you to make endless alterations and corrections and amendments in a blink of the eye – in fact to change your mind as often as you wish and virtually without cost. If you don't use a computer, there is always a cost in retyping that is quite out of proportion to the changes you make at any one time, and in the end you always end up offering work that could still be improved. With the computer you can simultaneously improve both the quantity and quality of your work, which in any other profession would be considered a miracle. The professional writer's computer of choice is the Apple Macintosh, which is comparatively expensive but makes up for the price by being easy to operate; most writers need only the cheapest model and those with journalistic or educational connections can get discounts.

BASIC CUTTING AND REWRITING

We shall not in this book consider cutting and rewriting as

separate activities. As you will by now have discovered, for the practising writer cutting and rewriting is a seamless, interchangeable process; the two tasks are only theoretically separable. However, a brief recap of cutting methods will give structure to the rest of our discussion of specific advanced cases that the professional writer sooner or later meets.

If you have recently read any books for novice writers, including mine, that contain the advice not to cut and rewrite until you have finished the book, forget it. Once you are on your third or fourth book, we can assume that you have enough experience to know when you are going wrong, that you have so much work that you don't want to waste time continuing in the wrong direction on the offchance of learning something new, and that you will not be so discouraged by the experience of going wrong that you will stop writing (an important reason for telling novices always to finish what they start, even if it goes off the rails halfway through).

It doesn't matter in what order you cut and rewrite, or how you tackle the task. The important thing is to finish the job, to be certain there are no unexamined words or implications left in your text when you deliver it. Any method that guarantees comprehensive review will work. My order is not necessarily better than yours, its sole purpose beyond the essential requirement of comprehensive review being to avoid wasting time by detailed work on sections that will later be cut in toto. It is therefore logical to start with the largest possible unit and work your way down to the smallest.

First, check that the structure of your story is sound; this specifically means that it should conform to the shortest possible complete chain of motivation. Lose all parts, books, chapters and sections that are unnecessary to the main story. Consider each subplot ultra-critically to see if it is essential or if it merely takes the reader on an irritating detour, away from the characters he loves. Any cut subplot also has ancillary sections that serve only the subplot: they too can go. Next shuffle what is left into different orders to see if you cannot by moving sections lose other large chunks and still retain a unified but shorter chain of motivation. All of this need not take very long but I always give it a whole week of careful attention because it is infuriating to do a lot of detail-work on a long section and then have an editor ask you to cut the whole thing.

When the structure is sound, work through with an eye primarily on cutting whole paragraphs that are superflous to the main action; these are normally descriptive and can usually go altogether or be replaced by a single linking phrase or even word. John Braine advised the writer not to describe the character walking upstairs unless he meets someone of interest on the stairs or sees something relevant to the action. This advice is pure gold; cut the paragraph of description and, if the transition cannot be made clear some other way, add to the first sentence of the next paragraph the single link-word, 'Upstairs...'

Next work through once more, cutting any sentences that are superfluous and have not yet caught your eye and been trashed on one of the other readings. On this reading I usually also break all sentences that need to be broken to clarify their meaning; this process usually points up parts of sentences, often qualifying phrases or compendium-lists, that can be chucked out.

Now we're down to the real nitty-gritty, where most cutting and rewriting time is spent, agonising over the value of a single word. For a start, you never need two adjectives and even one must justify its space. Don't be too hard on the adverbs though, unless you can replace the paired adverb and verb with a single stronger verb.

All this while you will be rewriting small pieces, a sentence here and a sentence there, and making notes on the manuscript to rewrite longer pieces or write new sections. The next stage is to write all the new material, then to cut it and to check by reading and shuffling that you have now achieved the correct chain of motivation.

If you can type at all, it helps your detail-work if you do your own retyping until the publisher's copy is actually being prepared. If you work with a computer, where you may be editing rather than retyping in total, always reformat to a different width: this helps to highlight the wrongness of words and phrases which may otherwise through being so tidily printed prematurely assume the authority of permanence.

The main rewriting can start anywhere but I normally do it from the beginning of the book to the end. The purpose is to ensure that each sentence says only what you want it to say and that no reader will receive from it any hidden meaning that you did not intend and, conversely, that every reader will comprehend both the overt message and the subtext that you do intend. Sentences which are overcomplicated, or which use wilfully obscure words, force the reader to work unnecessarily hard. Such sentences carry another kind of hidden meaning: that you have contempt for readers. At this stage many sentences will declare themselves candidates for cutting because you will find them difficult to rewrite into a form that makes their meaning crystal clear on first reading by the least of your readers. Don't sweat it: if the second time you try rewriting the sentence it doesn't come out right, the sentence is not earning its way and you can cut it.

Finally I read for phrases that may be exchanged for a single word. A great many common expressions slip too easily from speech into writing and appear to readers to be a careless waste of their time. 'Return' can almost always be substituted for 'come back', 'will' or 'shall' for 'am going to', and so on. How far you go in this direction depends on whom you are writing for: when I indicated that I would usually substitute 'trapezoid' for 'non-rectangular shape with four sides' I was accused by other writers of snobbishness but no bookbuyers complained when I actually did use 'trapezoidal' in one of my books.*

---

* A friend who speaks only perfect English and has in over sixty years never failed to make his meaning clear, did complain, but his copy was a gift in recognition of his help with the syntax of so many of my books. His point was that one may use such a word only if either the context or an inserted explanation makes the meaning clear. My defence was that the readers I aimed at would know the word or own a dictionary. With the advent of greater experience, I am now inclined to think he was right.

That's all there is to basic cutting and rewriting. Except that you should put the manuscript away for six months or so to gain the objectivity of distance and then go through the whole procedure again before sending the book to your publisher.

ADVANCED CUTTING AND REWRITING

Cutting and rewriting can be a creative act. It is true that most authors have to make a positive effort to arrive at the belief. However, if you cannot avoid doing the work, and no professional can, you may as well get maximum return for your effort. Cutting and rewriting can also cure some ills but those are, with very few exceptions, the result of mistakes that professional writers don't make, for instance an excess of autobiographical material. By the time the professional has finished his basic cutting and rewriting and is looking for that extra edge which separates the artist from the journeyman, the manuscript is in such good shape that it is almost impossible to distinguish between creative improvement or innovation and the correction of some very minor blemish. At this level, problems and opportunities wear the same mask.

The primest cut of all   Let's start with the largest possible disaster, a misfortune one would wish only on enemies not to be forgiven until they have been hanged; or, alternatively, an opportunity one would wish on none of one's friends. It sometimes happens that a professional writer produces a book that is perfect in its own terms but that no one wants. One possible reason for such a disaster is that the book was misconceived from the beginning. My novel *Festival*, in its original incarnation as a large tome on the arts in Australia, still stands in my memory as a perfect novel about the arts – and in the minds of my agents and publishers as an incredibly stupid waste of time, no matter what the internal evidence of its worth, because no one wanted it. It was saved from oblivion by a paperback editor who wanted a book from me fast and told me to throw away everything but the thriller subplot. Weirdly, the thriller subplot conveys more in its background about the arts in Australia than the big book from which it was extracted.

It is difficult to distinguish this problem from Duck's Disease: a book with Duck's Disease does not succeed even on its own terms because the author has never got to close quarters with his characters, whereas a book like the original version of my arts novel succeeds internally but fails to find a publisher because there isn't an audience for the subject. The fortunate author is the one whose publishers have the courage to refuse to publish it. The very fortunate author also has an editor who can tell him how to fix it – the author is usually too close to see that the subplot can be turned into a complete book. Even after it was explained to me, the process of cutting the main story hurt so much that instead I rewrote the subplot from beginning to end. Frankly, unless I know another writer very well indeed, I don't want to know him when this hardship befalls him, because it usually happens to the book he loves above all his other books and, what's worse, he wouldn't have written it if he hadn't in the first instance blinded himself to the commercial realities. Most professional writers know that it is a mistake for an author to jerk himself up on his creative dignity because commercial realities are cruel, but in many cases authors are not helped out of this pit because the potential helpers fear the explosion...

When the hurt has subsided after a good book is rejected, study its structure. After you throw out the main premise you may have something left, perhaps a second premise, perhaps a subplot, that can stand on its own and will convey at least something of your cherished message in a publishable form. A book in a bottom drawer never stops hurting but with *Festival* the half loaf turned into a pleasant surprise.

The habitual reader   Elsewhere we discussed your Ideal Reader, who is in all but the most unusual cases also an Habitual Reader. It is worth considering the habitual reader as a separate generic class when you tackle the final cutting and rewriting stages. Your ideal reader is so closely defined in terms of your own reading habits and preferences and prejudices that you are hardly likely to make a mistake in addressing him, but you never know who will pick up your book. If you have made a mistake in defining your ideal reader, that is no great setback as long as you have aimed too high in your expectations of your readers rather than too low. But you should be aware that all other readers who pick up any non-specialist book are likely to be habitual readers: two per cent of the people read ninety-eight per cent of the books.

The habitual reader is not defined by education or inherent intelligence but by familiarity with and unquestioning acceptance of general literary conventions. These are not the kind of literary conventions analysed in classrooms but something altogether subtler. The reader carries these conventions across the spectrum from Barbara Cartland to Graham Greene, from Judith Krantz to John Updike, from comic books to science fiction – this is the philosophical underpinning of the belief that even trash educates. The most important of these conventions for the process of cutting is that the author skips over periods when nothing happens. Next in importance is that he explains to the reader nothing more than is necessary at any stage of the narrative to understand the story. The implication is that most of the linking and establishing passages that so often vaguely irritate us even in books by professional authors should have been cut. If the author had read them with an habitual reader's eyes instead of a plotter's eyes he would have cut them. Blatant examples abound in non-fiction books by academics offered to the general public; one often wishes such scholars could be forced to write two versions, one for promotion committees to nitpick and another for real readers. One solution is to move establishing or explanatory material into appendices where the general reader can choose to give them a miss.

In our reading we routinely make mental leaps between sections of narratives, jumps from intention to deed, flights of implication from banal words; all these closures* depend

* See footnote on p70

161

less on intelligence or education than on the experience of having read something similar before, the residue of experience left by habitual reading. (Anyone who has ever worked with functional illiterates in a modern society knows how frustrating it can be to explain a story to someone who simply does not possess the assumptions that regular readers take for granted.) The habitual reader has been imprinted with certain expectations and only an arrogant fool would short-change him – or offend him by expounding on the obvious.

The professional writer would in the interest of economy have shrunk from writing superfluous material, so he should not under this head have to cut much on account of habitual readers. But critics too are habitual readers, and blasé ones at that. If you are one of those writers who feel that the opinion of critics is important, consider the habitual reader's tendency to leap from part to whole; trim your text rigorously so that you do not overtly make any link that is not absolutely essential. Critics appreciate the courtesy but I am certain most readers outside the literary establishment dislike writing that has been trimmed so much that they have to stop and consider what the characters would have done even if there is only one answer; that is going too far. A happy medium was suggested to me by a nursing nun of my aquaintance: 'I know a girl is disappointed when she is stood up. You don't have to explain that. But I want you to tell me how she told off the son of a bitch who did it.'

Younger writers, who grew up with television, are more inclined than older writers to cut too deep. On television the characterisation is instant even in good drama: the viewer likes the actor's face or he doesn't, and all the rest is development from that base. On television the action too is instant, carried by the audience's empathy with the actor much more than by pre-established motivational links; the viewer has seen the good guys and knows they will do the right thing. It is therefore important for writers who watch much television to understand that readers make a deliberate choice of books, and possibly of your book, because they want something more than the easy options of television. What they want, and what you can and should give them, is deeper characterisation, more thoroughly motivated action, 'people who act more real'. You can't do this if your book reads like a teleplay translated into stripped-down prose. Those who write prose like this in the first instance have the greatest difficulty in understanding that to habitual readers their material reads like second-rate comic books; they are probably best advised to stick to writing for the broadcast media. Real writers don't write stripped teleprose; they cut back to it. The risk of overdoing cutting isn't easy to avoid but with practice they can learn not to cut too deep; they could start by chucking out their television sets and immersing themselves for a few months in their favourite authors.

The test is always this: are you cutting into necessary characterisation? (The writers who should stick to broadcasting are content with minimal characterisation; they count on the rest of the team of director and actors to expand that into the characterisation that is necessary.) If the answer is yes, put it back, and a little more besides.

How to recognise the lean When you've cut all the fat, how do you know not to cut into the lean? The answer is to balance characterisation with pace. There is no reason to cut characterisation any deeper than the point where leaving the extra would interfere with the natural pace of the story. That is why I advise that you write for character but cut for pace. In the writing stages give the character all the space he needs because you know you can cut later, whereas it is almost impossible to come back and build up a character you have skimped, among other reasons because his character development may then take a different path and wreck your plot. There are genres in which readers have a high expectation of pace and these are becoming more and more difficult to write as readers' characterisation-expectations also increase; at the top of the market, novels of suspense are becoming longer to encompass both demands but the 'classic' detective story is still the same length it always was and even the best recent examples seem to be straining under the conflicting demands. You must make up your own mind where your best interests lie. For myself I have decided that where there is conflict between pace and necessary characterisation I shall give the space to the characterisation; the basis for my decision is that I believe the upward trend of demand for better characterisation will last.

The extra trim to the fillet   In the very last stages of your cutting and rewriting you should address the micro-elements of pace. It is extremely unlikely that with a properly planned and written book you should find any problem with the larger aspects of pace, the flow from the beginning of the tale accelerating towards the end. But you can still add an element of breathlessness by considering individual sentences and words. Sentences should be shorter, and beat to an accelerating rhythm, as they near the climax. Don't split sentences as you rewrite – cut the sections between the commas and after the semi-colons. Then check the build-up to your climax, and the climax itself, word for word, both for superfluity and the most economical choice of vocabulary; at the climax you should under no circumstances use any but active verbs.

TRICKS OF THE TRADE

On the way to the final active verb in your very last sentence you might have to consider a few technical aspects which may be more or less rare depending on the kind of work you do and perhaps on your personality.

Subbing the subplots   The professional writer of fiction is not likely to have problems with superfluous subplots: such subplots are normally the result of a lack of discipline he left behind in his novitiate. The professional novelist can spot a superfluous subplot at three miles even without his glasses and cuts it without compunction; we have already mentioned the subplot that should have been the novel, and below we shall return to subplots (and not only those of novelists) that can be recycled.

But subplots do give other creative writers, no matter how

professional, a great deal of difficulty. For some non-fiction writers the very demands of their professional status as scholars may erect barriers they must overcome to write readable books. An economic historian who once taught me divided writing into three classes: for peers, for students, for the public. But writing persuasively for all three classes at once is merely a matter of classification and arrangement. A little, a very little thought will suffice, said John Maynard Keynes. Once the writer has clearly in mind what he wants to say, all that remains is for him to decide which parts of his material will appeal to which sections of his audience and to arrange his book accordingly. We have already seen that appendices and postscripts can be used as a decent screen to protect the public from strictly scholarly material. But even scholarly material may be integrated into the body of a book by innovative design. In a large coffee-table book, for instance, the material for the general public can be placed as extended captions to the illustrations, that for students as the running text, the tables and other material strictly for experts as panels in a different typeface, and really dull stuff required by the promotions committee as appendices at the back of the book. Academic writers struck by this possibility should have a word with their publishers very early in the planning stages of the book if they wish to avoid a great deal of rewriting later.

Specialist technical expertise and the critics Academics and other writers in highly technical fields can of course never have too much expertise; we have already said enough about communicating with a more general public and they can therefore skip to the next subhead. But specialist technical expertise is dangerous to the serious novelist because of a snobbery inherent in literary circles; the more mechanical the technical expertise, the more reprehensible it is to display it, the more philosophical or theoretical (excluding higher mathematics and physics) the more acceptable. This is another point where your editor and publisher are not likely to be reliable guides. Most editors read so much that from pure boredom they are likely to pounce on any technical expertise you have as a novelty that they can exploit; in fairness, many books based around expertise in, say, submarines have been very successful with the public precisely because the author knew what he was talking about. However, in any novel that is likely to get serious attention an excess of technical detail is dangerous because critics are certain to pick on it as an easy target. My novels *Sinkhole* and *Iditarod* attracted small but tiresome adverse comment – the barb in the tail of the praise – because, I must presume, novelists are not supposed to know about mountain rescue or sled dog racing in the Arctic. By way of comparison my novel *The Zaharoff Commission*, which absolutely turns on the economic condition of Germany in June 1918 ('a masterful study of a feudal society in terminal fracture under pressure of inflation' said a scholarly magazine), attracted only favourable comment even though the level of economic expertise displayed is not only at a higher pitch than the survival expertise in the other two novels but present in much greater quantities.*

There's not much you can do about this danger, except to restrain your publishers from leading you astray. If five per cent of your expertise on a subject shows above the waterline, that is about right, leaving ninety-five per cent to illuminate your book indirectly.

Or you may decide you are a technofreak yourself, so bugger the critics and let it all hang out. In this case you'd better stick to science fiction or suspense or the more forensic police procedurals, where technical expertise is properly valued.

Overly balanced books   The narrative must be complete, we have agreed that. But does it have to be tidy? Life is not tidy or particularly symmetrical except in the very long term, which is why the book with an artificial tidiness offends some inexplicable aesthetic sense. This fault is particularly prevalent in novels, perhaps because it is so easy to achieve;

---

* I am by training an economist and motivational psychologist and just couldn't resist showing off.

but sometimes non-fiction writers too try for the perfectly closed book, the one in which there are not only no loose ends (no professional writer's book should have loose ends except by design) but no rough edges. This is a self-defeating ambition, because what attracts us to characters is essentially their idiosyncrasies, their very rough edges; and what attracts us to a story is its novelty, the very unexpectedness and unevenness of its progress. If you are tempted to force a rounded tidiness on your story, read a few old Agatha Christies and note how she imposes reality on her tale by resisting the temptation to knock off those rough corners and provide us with a fully closed ending (where, especially for detective fiction writers, the temptation is great). One example of unnatural tidiness particularly irritates me: books which follow the Victorian moralistic convention that justice always triumphs, in which the bad guys not only get their comeuppance but every bad guy gets his desserts in perfectly strict proportion to the degree of evil he has committed – even the most Olympian judge from the world's greatest democracy would not believe that such a depiction has the remotest connection with real life.

In the example above the offence is blatant and bad in itself because it rejects common sense and common experience, but the overly-balanced narrative also has the much more insidious effect of destroying subtlety throughout your book.

You can provide yourself with a shield against the too-tidy book by sincerely striving for realism and making an effort not to force your personal moral precepts on your characters.

If you find you have committed this sin, look first to your ending, where a few small cuts of superfluous material may save your whole book because that is usually where the evidence is strongest. Cuts will probably also be required elsewhere and in really bad cases substantial rewriting.

The loose character   This is actually a perfectly integrated character whose actions and characteristics you can with profit transfer to another character. By the stage of polish we have now achieved this character is rooted like a tree in a landscape, and is as difficult to spot because you have been glaring at the forest too long. The character will not read 'thin' – if by this stage any of your characters is not fully fleshed, you have a disaster on your hands – but by comparison with other characters of the same weight he will seem to be slightly less well rounded. What's more, there will normally be another character who suffers from the same relative undernourishment. By definition (again, at this stage of your book's development), such characters will not be major but middleweights or minor-league players. Normally they will be on the same side, angels or black hats. What I do when I have discovered them is to fold one character into the other, to give the surviving character the actions and characteristics of the other as well as his own; this requires rewriting all the scenes in which the new and bigger character appears but it results in the most interestingly varied, sometimes even tortured, characters. You have to search for this opportunity because it is far too subtle to hit you in the face, but the result is worth the effort. Putting the manuscript away for some months can lend perspective.

Too much pace   Many thriller-writers will deny there is such an animal as a book too quick-paced for habitual thriller readers and that may be true; I love Jack Higgins because his books are all pace. But in every other genre the reader now and again needs time to think, to draw a breath, to gird himself for the next climax. Even in the longer novel of suspense, with its multi-layered climaxes, too much pace can wreck the cyclical rhythm of the book.

The real problem with the over-paced book is that the pace is achieved at the expense of characterisation. Too much pace is therefore always a dire warning of something fundamentally wrong with a narrative. When it occurs, you should be on guard for missing links in the chain of motivation and for serious shortfalls in the characterisation. Don't just 'write in a breathing break', as one admittedly inexperienced editor instructed me; check the whole thing with an ultra-critical eye against all the fundamental requirements we have canvassed.

Style By now you will have created a book in your own distinctive style. Arnold Bennett used to feel sorry for people who asked him to teach them literary style because, he said, they didn't understand that style cannot be taught, style being merely having something to say and saying it plainly. But it was poor Arnold Bennett who missed the point, that at an earlier time, lost in the quicksands of his memory, he had taught himself to 'say it plainly'. Style cannot be taught – to others. But you can teach yourself. Once you have said it plainly, don't be tempted to add 'literary' flourishes; they will merely make your work read like the output of those writers who follow the fashion because they have nothing worthwhile to say.

Waste not, want not Any subplot you cut should be put aside and examined later to ascertain whether it will make a book. Any character you cut, especially a major character, should be put aside and examined later to determine whether he suggests a theme for a whole book. All large sections you cut, especially if you are a non-fiction writer who sticks to one field of interest, should be saved and filed for future use; it is amazing how often, three books hence, you remember that a piece you threw out expressed exactly what you now want to say.

7
DEVELOPING THE WRITER'S PERSONALITY
BLOCKS AND ATTITUDES

A writer writes. A professional writer writes every day of a set working week; most of the ones I know write something even on weekends.

The mechanical limitations of the keyboard (or speaking speed for those few writers who dictate) make writing a desperately slow business. Writing with a pen or pencil is even slower. Thought is of course timeless but imposing order on the result of the mental process takes a great deal of time. Furthermore, writing is a craft that most commonly proceeds by trial and error even in the hands of experts of very long standing; the trial and error of repeated cutting and rewriting is by definition time-consuming. The professional writer's desire for perfection can also swallow huge amounts of time for improvements others may think marginal or unnecessary.

The first imperative of the professional writer is therefore to arrange his life so as to schedule the proper amount of time for his writing and all its ancillary conceptual activities, of which the chief one is time to think. The proper amount is usually the same as the maximum time that he can spend productively at his work before fatigue sets in. It doesn't matter much if you answer letters and attend to the auxiliary work like filing and checking royalty statements when your mental edge has been blunted by a long day of creative work, but writing beyond a certain point can appeal only to an audience of wastebaskets.

The second imperative for the professional writer is to consider and accept some conscious scheme of work so that his necessarily limited time is used to maximum effect. He does this by establishing daily routines and physical and mental habits that prevent time being wasted unproductively in what the historian Paul Johnson calls 'circular thinking'.

If you somehow arrived on the verge of professionalism without discovering the necessary routines and attitudes, you may decide not to tamper with your present successful if not necessarily optimal methods, given of course that they are methods and not just blind luck. Alternatively you can read the chapter in *Start Writing Today!* which deals with the routines of a professional writer. The same chapter explains why blocks are the psychosomatic diseases of hypochondriac authors, and lists ways of preventing blocks ever happening to a writer through good planning, sound routines and, above all, attention to understanding his characters. There is a more specialised and higher-level chapter on the same subject in my *Writing a Thriller*. Here we will assume that a writer with two or three publishable books completed has learned the right routines and attitudes either the hard way or through reading some reliable guide; we will therefore address much more advanced methods and considerations.

Error! Error! Error!   Many authors – Gore Vidal, for instance – are enraged by the mere mention of blocks; in their view, claims of being blocked are no more than the excuses of poseurs and dilettantes for shortfalls of talent or, worse, sneering exhibitions of laziness or, worst of all, gloating declarations of scorn for the craft which underpins communication. If one defines a block as a psychological impediment to achieving the best work an artist is capable of, or a psychological barrier to doing any work at all, all professional writers must agree with the scoffers. However, if one uses the word 'block' as shorthand for the visible symptom of a failure of one of the multitude of complex tasks an author must perform before he can write confidently, it can be a useful concept. Because 'block' has such a baggage-train of entirely unacceptable pseudo-psychiatric connotations, I prefer the less emotive and more precise image of a red-lit box on the wall flashing *Error! Error! Error!*

When the writer arrives at a point where he cannot continue writing, it is in no circumstances whatsoever due to a psychological condition peculiar to the creative personality. To believe that it is to fall into the wretched Ruskinite fallacy that the artist is somehow different from (the Ruskinites like to read 'better than') other people. More, where it isn't an excuse for inactivity or wallowing in flattering self-pity ('How I suffer for my art!'), it is a temptation to treat the symptom rather than the disease, which in turn is to invite the problem to return – frequently. In reality the condition is a cold warning from your brain to your fingers that some-where along the way you fouled up the mechanical task of building links in a chain. It is the creative craftsman's equiv-alent of the flashing light on the wall at Mission Control in Houston and it can save an author a great deal of time if he considers it as an engineering warning of an impending failure rather than anything more profoundly 'creative'.

We have considered many examples throughout this book of occasions where a writer would arrive at a narrative point and know something was wrong because it didn't feel right to continue; in each case we could offer as the root cause a failure of preparatory work, usually in fully understanding the motivations of his characters. These blocks provide splendid opportunities for those masochists who wish to suffer for their art to condemn their books and their careers to the dustbin of history. The professional writer with the right attitude wastes no time feeling sorry for himself but turns immediately to curing the underlying cause – to repeat, in almost all instances a failure to understand his characters fully – so that he may continue with his work.

There are no blocks.

Attitudes are money   It would be wrong to say that for a writer time is money: it is obvious that much of the best writing is so well done because the author never considered the miserable hourly rate he could expect even if the book were successful. The author who believes time is money is either a hack or has so firmly repressed his better instincts that it surely must hurt – in which case he should switch to a profession where his capabilities would be financially better rewarded. However, that is not a licence for a writer to waste time which could otherwise be applied to writing more or writing better.

Proper work routines are evidence of the right attitude. When Bernard Sher-Cliff travelled three thousand miles to meet me after contracting for my first book, his questions about my work routines were downright rude. They were not designed to protect his investment, but to discover whether I would survive the long haul as an author or had merely hit a lucky single shot; he wasn't so much investigating when and how I worked as whether there was a routine in place. The existence of a routine guarantees a professional approach. Since then, all my books including my novels have, against the received wisdom of publishing, been commissioned, not so much because of a faultless batting average (a writer with a perfect score is one who never took a risk) but because publishers know an author with the right attitude will somehow make the time to do all the necessary cutting and rewriting on every book. If you have the right attitude, make sure your publisher knows it – it is, quite literally, worth money in the bank.*

When you've really dried up Let's switch gears here, from talking about books you have in progress to the ones you would like to write or have to write to pay the bills but discover with horror you have no subject for. This has never happened to me, partly because I have a routine for storing ideas until they are required, as described earlier, but it

---

* Until you have at least ten published books to your name, always, without fail, when you offer or deliver one book mention in a brief sentence each the book in the drawer awaiting cutting and rewriting, the one currently on your typewriter, and the one you have in planning, even if all three have been pre-sold to other publishers. Besides the obvious benefit of creating advance interest, or eliciting advice that you are flogging a dead horse if the publisher knows you well, or perhaps even an offer and an advance subject to the book turning out as you promise, this casts on you the golden glow of a continuing, professional, working author. Even writers of long standing often fail to appreciate how highly publishers rate continuity.

happens routinely to many other professional writers. Even those with files full of ideas could fail at a given moment to be inspired by anything in the file. At this stage there is a source of ideas available only to writers with one or more books behind them, books not necessarily published but good enough to have attracted the attention of a publisher or editor, who will consequently have opened a dialogue with the writer. The writer can then ask the editor if he has any ideas or pet schemes looking for an author. In fact, if an author is only a little more established, editors and publishers offer him ideas whether he needs them or not. A third of Andrew McCoy's books originated in themes offered by publishers. My New York agent, in discussion with publishers about a possible deal, was on one day offered two unsolicited sets of four ideas each for me to develop – more than half of them exciting concepts and the rest by no means dross. For the writer establishing himself as a professional the advantage of accepting an idea from an editor is that it carries with it a built-in bias to acceptance and publication because the editor wouldn't propose ideas lacking in marketing clout and he wouldn't waste his pets on a writer incapable of handling the book.

It is inadvisable to ask for ideas if you have anything of your own going or any prospect of finding an idea of your own; by the nature of things your own ideas are always superior – to you anyway – and there is no point in offending an editor by letting his ideas lie fallow in your care.

A WRITER'S HUMAN PROBLEMS

A writer has no special problems that other professionals do not also have. Even the more specialised of his concerns are shared with other types of creative artists and the majority of interpretative artists. Moreover, he has much in common with vast armies of craftsmen and absolute hordes of the self-employed, from carpenters to insurance agents. We have already dismissed the possibility that the writer has a special, different psyche which creates its own problems. However, it is worth rolling even well-stubbed stones from the path of progress, especially now that so many writers come into the trade straight from college without first experiencing another profession in which they could acquire adaptive skills from peers and mentors; the change is important because writing is a solitary occupation which offers, compared with almost any other profession, very few opportunities to learn ancillary skills from those who went before.

Loneliness Norman Mailer's claim that the occupational disease of writers is alcoholism is an excuse as much as it is a self-advertisement. It is about as true as claiming that the occupational disease of policemen is suicide when a very little thought will uncover the truth: a policeman's suicide is a symptom of the despair and futility engendered by too much contact with the dregs of humanity. The occupational disease of writers is loneliness; the heraldic emblem of the professional writer is the plain white wall he faces all day long. Writers are no more alcoholic than other classes of professionals with similar incomes and stresses, nor even statistically as likely to become alcoholic as others with lonely jobs. However, alcohol is a danger for some writers. A Grand Old Man of our profession, himself no mean imbiber after working hours, advised me to move the liquor tray out of my study because, he said, he could date the decline in the work of several writers he knew intimately from the time the tray with bottles and glasses became a permanent fixture at their elbows; he added that any writer whose dust jacket photographs include a bottle or a glass is almost always beyond redemption. All of this is true, once you know what to look for, but libel laws and common decency prevent me from naming examples. Another author's wife told me a time came when she would lock her husband's study door and not give him a drink until he had written a thousand words; those were the only thousand words he wrote on any day. It's just as well that by this time they weren't worrying about where their next meal came from. Even best sellers cannot live in the manner to which they have accustomed themselves on a thousand words a day because that leaves no space for errors, for essential cutting and rewriting; in fact, only a fool would assume that a writer with a permanent hangover could knock off a thousand good words five days a week.

A fellow with a humdrum administrative job may perhaps operate on autopilot week after week but an alert mind is in my experience as necessary to the writer as it is to the racing driver or pilot or filmmaker or advertising executive who wants to do decent work.

Alcohol and other drugs are only the most common danger of the isolation inseparable from the author's profession. Mental imbalance can in extreme cases result, though psychiatrists tend to attribute this less to loneliness than to the effects of obsession. I think they are wrong: we can agree that writers are driven to obsession both by their urge for perfection and by their compassion, but we must not overlook the extent to which isolation is a powerful breeder of obsession, especially in the absence of counterbalancing daily contact with your fellows in a normal working environment (say an office). But this is only the most extreme reason for an author to set aside some time for social activities: the most basic one of keeping in touch with people, the source of all his characters, is professionally far more important. What you do depends on your circumstances and your personality but a time will come when you will have to make an effort to build up some social life; it is best to consider it a necessity and set aside the required time right at the start of your career. Social intercourse is a habit you lose if you don't practise.

Insecurity   Writing is an insecure profession, both financially and psychologically. The first consideration is not to do something to ameliorate these problems, but to ensure that they do not wreck your career. Financial insecurity often drives authors to push for deals that publishers can only reject, or resent even when they acquiesce, or that are certain to result in large unearned advances. Psychological insecurity makes writers recklessly demanding of publishers' time and limited emotional resources, another cause of resentment. Authors have to guard consciously against these excesses because they can wreck a writer's career as surely as a carelessly written book.

To some extent you can cushion yourself against financial insecurity by saving when you can. I don't, but then I am an optimist with experience of the advantages of living on the edge gained in motor racing, advertising and other high-rolling professions; you may prefer a more sedate life. A proper concern for your publishers' livelihood also in time confers a modest security. It never pays to wring the last cent from a publishing deal, because next year it might be the straw that breaks the camel's back just as you want to nego-tiate a new book. If a publisher wants to renegotiate a signed contract, I always agree with any reasonable request; normally the publisher wants me to take the base rather than the escalated royalty so that a small reprint can keep the book in print. The alternative is to stand on your contractual rights, say no, let the book go out of print, take the rights back, and lose the publisher.

The time may come when you yourself want to renegotiate a contract long since signed. With several of my publishers I have asked for and received back free of charge subsidiary rights (required for package deals to other media or to terri-torially distant publishers) that were contractually theirs; they could hardly refuse when I could point to my acquies-cence in the small reprints. On another occasion when a publisher hated a book he had commissioned and paid for, instead of forcing him to publish or give the book back so that I could resell it and so be paid twice*, I allowed him to

---

* The word 'acceptance' on a publisher's contract is ambiguous in that the publisher can, and often will, claim that the publication of a commissioned book is within his discretion, or that such books must at least be provably suitable for publication by his firm; entertainment lawyers, however, are of the opinion that once the author has a contract, a book may be found unacceptable by a publisher only if it is unpub-lishable. I avoid this problem by having all reference to acceptance struck from my contracts except in regard to making all final advance payments due within six weeks of delivery. This leaves the publisher his powerful common law right of rejecting inferior goods: the upshot is that a publisher who rejects a book gets his money back if you cannot prove it is publishable by selling it to another house for the same advance or better, and loses his money if you do sell it to another house. You should not sign contracts containing clauses, intended to protect publishers from their own errors of judgement, forcing you to repay if they reject a publishable book. But a rigid stand on contractual rights will not in the long term benefit your career. Several years later, when the firm under discussion above imported a new management whom I already knew well, I was shown a memo written at the time of the disastrous book which noted a decision to let me go; it had not crossed the mind of anyone on the editorial board that an author would behave well in such circum-stances, and the only possible conclusion was that the relationship was at an end.

sell the book to another publisher and thereby recover his advance plus a share in the profits; he promptly gave me a roll-over contract in which he commissioned two novels, with a new one commissioned as soon as I delivered the first, so that I could always plan two books ahead. More, in the middle of a bitter argument about the subject of my next book with the chief editor of this house, its publisher, hearing that I had big legal expenses fighting an attempt to suppress one of my books, sent me a cheque with a note to the effect that it was an advance against a book for which we would discuss a subject and draw up a contract whenever I next had time to think. An author-publisher relationship is not a one-shot make or break affair but continues as long as both parties can profit; make sure your publisher realises you understand this – and you will have taken the sharpest edge off the financial insecurity of your profession.

Psychological insecurity is not so easy. There is a school of thought which believes artists are insecure because they are artists, or even that they are artists because they are insecure; either view is nonsensical. A far more credible explanation for the very common occurrence of feelings of insecurity in artists is that most of the causes are environmental, financial insecurity being a very large environmental factor. Other elements of the ambience in which writers operate contribute weightily enough to insecurity to make it impossible to eliminate the problem merely by giving writers money. Soviet writers before perestroika were among their society's most privileged citizens but other environmental factors unbalanced them quite visibly, the most notable being the fear inspired by the possibility of official disapproval of their writing. Television comedy writers commonly work in teams not as a refuge from loneliness but to spread the stress of being funny while an immovable deadline threatens; they are very well paid but I have never met or heard of one who is not insecure.

The publishing industry has its own insecurity-breeding mechanisms even when no cancer has grown on it (see below about the shit endemic to a life in the arts). The writer may be able to ally himself to a firm small enough for him to have a personal relationship with the head of the house, or at least with one editor who deals with all his books and concerns; such houses are few and far between and, precisely because they are small, much pickier than the big boys about whom they take on; once you are in, however, you are often in for life. Or you may be fortunate enough to have 'grown up' with an editor who has over the years become a big shot in one of the big multinationals. I still have a good relationship with my very first paperback editor, with whom I am now at the fourth firm where he has worked in fifteen years, though these days he publishes a thousand books every year instead of a hundred-odd. Every other writer has to deal with the unacceptable face of conglomeration, which accounts for the fact that authors now try to have it written into their contracts that they can move with their editors when they leave for another publisher; finding a really good editor is such a rare event that most authors don't get lucky more than once or twice in a lifetime.

Before the writer finds that editor, there are plenty of opportunities to be made insecure by the processes of modern publishing. The number of independent houses is being reduced annually: that gives the individual author fewer chances to have his book accepted (never mind the narrowing of scope and the dearth of independent minds willing and able to take a chance on something novel). Your book might not be read at all because some houses accept manuscripts only from agents; the few first-rate agents don't want to take on newcomers, while the second-rate agents have abdicated their responsibility of judging what can be sold by demanding that potential clients show 'at least three appearances in the little magazines' (which are an utter waste of a professional writer's time). At some houses your book might be read only by someone very junior and, depending on her taste or the state of her nail-enamel, be bucked upstairs or returned to you. At other houses you must target your submission precisely or it may well come back without being seen by the correct editor for your type of book. I sent copies of a proposal (together with a list of my published books so that there could be no mistaking my serious intent) to six divisional chiefs in one of the world's largest publishers. Later I asked the man who finally made me an offer for the book how many copies had reached his division. I was staggered to discover that he had received only the copy addressed directly to him – and I wouldn't have known about his brand-new division if Anne Watts of A. & C. Black (who publish the annual *Writers' and Artists' Yearbook*) hadn't mentioned it might be a home for my book. We can go on, but there's no point. The remedy is to get a good agent, or preferably more than one agent if you are prolific or write in more than one field, because even for agents publishing is now so difficult and complex that the best ones tend to specialise.

Even when your book is accepted and paid for, insecurity is the inevitable byproduct of many modern practices. For instance, copy-editing standards have declined radically since I became a writer twenty years ago (one of my agents says, 'A writer should not send in a book that requires copy-editing'), yet more and more firms no longer send galleys to authors for correction and approval, so that they publish over your name whatever the compositor sees fit to set. Unless your contract states quite specifically that you will see galleys (not page-proofs, on which change is prohibitively expensive), do not make a single handwritten alteration on your manuscript because it will surely be misinterpreted. Very few firms now show you the jacket design of your books until the plates have been made and all the covers printed and laminated; I have a tender spot for the London publisher Robert Hale because they still send out sketch designs of their jackets for the author's approval before proceeding to finished art, and their many other courtesies are legendary. As for jacket copy, which used to be written by an editor who had actually read your book (and at Secker in days of yore was often written in my presence by the publisher himself), that is now written by copywriters who get a summary of the story on a briefing sheet and by PR people from the bio-info sheet the writer is asked to fill in; I was told recently that I must be the last author who still writes his own cover copy for his paperbacks – 'and that's only permitted because you were once a famous advertising copywriter.' As for control over paper quality (relevant to some books), print quality (relevant to a technical book on colour-print production I want to do), or a sensible typeface and size (relevant to not getting a thick ear from readers who write that they won't buy your next book because this one was set in an unreadable size), forget it.

These are small matters, but you have even less control over bigger matters. When I complained to one publisher about the lack of promotion for my book, and backed up my complaint with proof of publicity and sales for the same book in another country where I had taken care of the matter myself precisely because I knew a complaint without supporting evidence would be brushed off, he got rid of the PR director and appointed an even bigger incompetent to the job – and then had the cheek to blame me for leaving him in a worse position than before. Many of the better publishers will, if the writer approaches them right, refund any expenses he incurs in handling publicity for his book. But only a few writers are proficient in organising such matters (as opposed to merely turning up for an interview organised by someone else) and in any event they shouldn't have to do it.

Finally, even if the publishing firm fulfils its major responsibilities, the larger the firm the more likely the writer is to have his insecurity quotient increased by the small discourtesies of big organisations: editors in meetings whenever he calls, telephone calls not returned because the message slips went missing, editors working at home to get something done (and I don't want to have to call them at home even when invited to do so), junior nobodies who treat writers like lesser nobodies, idiot receptionists and the other minor irritations of doing business with big business. The only consolation is that it is as bad for everyone else who has to deal with conglomerates – the reason writers notice so much is that they are largely protected from the everyday experience of John Citizen.

For those readers who fancy themselves philosophers, here's a universal publishing riddle: why does it take a publisher nine months to respond yes or no to a proposal that takes three minutes to read?

'The shit endemic to a life in the arts' William Goldman not only gave us *Butch Cassidy and the Sundance Kid* and that fine growing-up novel *The Color of Light*, he brought us the bright idea that if you call unacceptable behaviour shit, you expose it for what it is. What we are discussing here is not shortcomings beyond the control of those whom writers have to deal with, but failings that a little thought and natural courtesy could mend.

Don't start out believing that writers get the shortest end of the stick. The shit endemic to a life in the arts is spread unevenly over the arts, and, in truth, very thinly over writers and painters, who are in the main in charge of their own destinies in that they can keep working even when no one wants their work. Actors, on the other hand, lead truly awful lives because they are so dependent on others and spend most of their time waiting to be offered parts.

A writer has to put up with a spectrum of loutishness. Book publishing, where the majority of writers have most or all of their contact with the commercial world, is at the nicer end by far though conditions are deteriorating as publishers become more and more executives of large conglomerates rather than readers-become-editors-become-publishers. Two examples of thoughtlessness will suffice. One publisher sent out with all rejected manuscripts xeroxed information about a bureau that offered a rewrite service, which is an insult even to the rank novice and infuriating to those several authors they sent it to who each had more books in print than the combined lifetime output of all the so-called writers in the rewrite bureau – besides, if the rewriters were so good, how come they weren't writing their own books? One can easily understand that receipt of this missive by a novice, who probably does not know how to discover that the publisher sent it out with every rejected manuscript, will induce a major crisis of confidence in his own skill. Such stupidity contributes nothing to developing any writer; it is an insult to the intelligence of the whole publishing community. It almost makes one want to praise those firms who send out preprinted rejection cards. My second example concerns a middle-aged writer who had won every prize offered for his genre three times or more, had an international reputation both in the genre and as a straight novelist under another name, and whose books had on numerous occasions made lasting films that were also commercially successful. While not rich, he had made a decent life for himself and his family from his writing. Yet this man was told by a power-executive, thirty years his junior and imported from the mother company to be a dealmaker, that, 'We will start establishing your reputation as soon as you sign this long-term contract with us.' The worst thing, according to the writer, was that the worsted suit wasn't being deliberately discourteous: he simply didn't know he was being outrageously insulting. (How can there be a meeting of minds between a man who measures his reputation by the respect of his peers and readers and another who measures it only in dollars?) After that, says the writer, 'talk of an author being "a commodity no different from soap powder" just washed over me.' He signed, because there was no alternative, and banked their money. Then he had his lawyer find a loophole in the contract and deliberately sold one of his books that escaped through it to another publisher to run a spoiling operation. Good for him.

At the other end of the shit spectrum are the majority of film production companies; the honourable exceptions are mainly small companies, or decent individuals in the big faceless organisations. One writer objected to a producer calling the actors 'meat' and was told, 'You're just meat too, and sit a long way below the salt.' Most insults to writers in film writing are not quite so literate. Writers come a long way down the totem pole: their work is rewritten without consultation not only by actors but by script girls; I once had a scene substantially amended by an electrician too lazy to change the lights to suit the dialogue as written – and I discovered the rewrite only when a rival union objected. But many writers with film ambitions are terminally discouraged by the difficulty of even getting their scripts read. Sometimes one wonders if film companies are rude on purpose, as a sort of initiation test. One self-important halfwit at a film company returned an unsuitable book of mine with a note that she was 'not a free reading service'. If she had any sense, she should have told me what she was looking for; not long after she was fired, her successor asked why I never offered his firm anything and took options on two of my properties that were suitable for his company.

These are by no means isolated examples. The legal release many film companies expect you to sign before they will read your material is a licence to steal and you should have it checked by an entertainments lawyer.* A film contract is another licence to steal. The film industry's notion of their expenses allowable against gross income to arrive at the net profit, on which your cut will be based, is a travesty of sound accounting practice; the so-called 'producer's profit', of which a writer might be offered a larger cut, is an even lesser amount, usually negative. Female writers in films are subject to substantial sexual pressure. Rubber cheques and ludicrous contingency offers ('give me an option for a dollar now and I'll make your fortune when I bank the movie') can waste a lot of a writer's time and emotional resources; if a producer who has trashed my time before calls me direct, I ask for a goodwill fee of a couple of thousand dollars before I even listen to him. The best answer is a tough agent.

A word to the new professional writer: most films don't get made, to such an extent that down the road here one writer lives in a grand house overlooking Courtmacsherry Bay on the proceeds of having written seven films that were never produced. Unless you intend to be a full-time film writer, take the option money and run; carry on with your next book rather than becoming involved in the film's development. Writers who are personally sensitive, or who believe that the exact form of their work is important (as opposed to the overall shape and message), should stay clear of films. Joe Esterhas received three million dollars for a feature script,

---

* Refusal to sign, or using a release amended to give you some protection, is not really the answer either. One film company stole ten out of twelve telefeature ideas from a set of thumbnails I prepared. This was too large a correspondence of subject matter for coincidence but not quite large enough to take legal action because the thumbnails were too short for detailed comparison – here the answer would have been expansive outlines.

wrote an article for the New York *Times* on how powerful writers had now become in the film industry – and three weeks later was fired from the film.

Television, too, splits rather neatly into two very different parts. TV funded from the public purse is usually much easier to break into than the commercial kind. We have commented elsewhere on how pleasant and instructive it is to work with Britain's BBC (but not Channel 4, where they have an overblown estimation of their own importance) and I have had good reports about the Australian ABC and Canadian CBC. But commercial television companies throw up the same barriers and permit themselves the same arrogant behaviour as the film producers; in many cases they are the same organisations. There are still a few places in the world where commercial television producers will read your 'un-agented' script and from these you will usually get a reasonable contract; besides the publicly funded television stations, I have experience or knowledge of a handful of British and Australian commercial networks which treat writers like people. All the rest should be approached with a tough lawyer at your side unless you like being ripped off in a manner so blatant the insult seems calculated. Again, an agent is virtually essential.

The theatre at its peak is another meatmarket, not much different from films. One playwright tells of walking into a New York restaurant and greeting a husband-and-wife producing team who had lost $800,000 on a play of his three years before – and he had to tell them his name twice before they remembered who he was! But just below the highest level, if you can take the shit, you can get in. We'll pass lightly over those ensembles where actors are allowed, in some cases encouraged, to change your work to suit their own personalities... Be prepared to lose every battle because your ego is unlikely to be a match for those you will find even in the tackiest of provincial theatres, to be blamed when decisions you were clearly opposed to lead to disaster, to be forced to be unpleasant to recover your full share of the takings, and to receive no share in the credit for any success. One of my fondest memories of the gifted playwright Steve J. Spears is of him tucked away in the theatre holding his girlfriend's hand while on the stage the director and actors and producer and stage designer and ticket collector took their bows after the première of one of his hit plays.

Lowest common denominator   Critics are the chemical fertiliser of all the creative professions: the majority contribute nothing to creative growth and most are unacceptably poisonous. The average standard of literary criticism is much lower than in any of the other representational or performing arts, perhaps because there are so many literary critics that the few good ones cannot pull the average up to a respectable level.* William Goldman notes that if the film is good, critics believe the director did it all himself, but if it turns out less than perfect the writer wrecked the director's film! So what else is new?

We all know about the coteries of writers and critics who review each other's books, and give each other grants and prizes; this isn't new. If it bothers a writer he can always channel his energy into breaking into the charmed circle rather than actually writing. Some writers never read what the critics have to say on the justified ground that most criticism is simply stupid. A prime example of critical stupidity happened to me a few years ago when I had two books published in New York in the same week and reviewed in a leading magazine. On one page a critic praised the book under my own name far beyond its true deserts mainly, I suspect, because it was too difficult for him to understand; its wit and elegance were favourably remarked on. On the opposite page a novel published under a pseudonym was slammed for 'involuntary humour' (now that's a talent I'd love to have! – perhaps this critic could also arrange for me to write my books involuntarily, say while I sleep) and the style was excoriated as barely competent. On the other side of the Atlantic the two books were reviewed a fortnight apart

---

* To declare my interest: I used to write on the performing and representational arts and am now a novelist. However, these views are held in common with many of the leading critics in all fields who fear that the reputation of their craft will be damaged by the efflorescence of incompetent comment on the arts.

in the leading British literary publication and the treatment meted out was reversed, a perfect mirror image; the British view was probably the correct evaluation of these books and certainly bookbuyers and library borrowers have concurred ever since.

That newspapers should hire stupid critics is an insult to writers but one they must perforce bear in silence.

When the media hire incompetent critics, failed writers, those with a personal bias, or crooks, I don't believe writers should suffer in silence. However, it is inadvisable to write letters for publication to the paper because they will invariably in their response present you as a curmudgeon and a whiner. But there is more than one way to skin a cat. My novel *Reverse Negative* was reviewed favourably in every major newspaper in the world except one; the single adverse review appeared in a key paper in a city where I had once lived. It reviewed the dustjacket blurb and my biographical detail most unfavourably; the story itself was briefly dismissed; and then the critic turned approvingly to 'two little books' from a publisher I had never heard of. Discreet enquiries elicited the information that the critic in question had a manuscript under consideration by the publisher of the two 'little books'; more, though his name rang no bells, I had once thrown him into a politician's swimming pool for being intolerably rude to our hostess. Here then was a case of an incompetent who reviews the dust jacket instead of the book, of a failed writer, and of personal bias, not to mention the dishonesty of his attempt to ingratiate himself with a likely publisher of his own book. I did nothing about it – until two years later when I arranged for both the literary editor and the features editor (a far more important person to the finances of a newspaper because his section attracts real advertising rather than the mickey mouse spending of publishers and booksellers) to be invited on a first-class freebie trip to an arts festival. Here I gave them a lavish lunch at the expense of one of my publishers and laid out the evidence, explaining how the reputation of their paper would be damaged if such a happening was blown up out of proportion by a rival newspaper chain. Not waiting until they got home, they fired the critic by phone that afternoon. Of course most writers, being nice people from honest backgrounds, would not know how to put in this kind of fix* – and shouldn't be forced to learn. But very few writers who have spent longer than a decade in the business do not have a similar story of critical incompetence, bias, or crooked self-interest (even if not such a compounded and blatant case); in most instances they suffered in silent frustration for lack of the tools to strike back at their tormentors.

Then there is the political critic, who damns your novel not for its merits or lack of them but because he disagrees with what he assumes are the author's politics. There is no recourse; you just have to wear it. If you want to be well reviewed in that man's paper, you must twist your narrative to conform to his world-view.

Nor can you strike back at the critic who simply fails to understand what your book is about, even if every other critic is of the opinion that you overachieved your targets. It is impossible to prove that his mistake stems from stupidity rather than an honest difference of opinion. And you wouldn't want to suppress honest free speech, would you?

There is one thing writers can and should do to lessen the amount of bad and spiteful criticism: they should not become literary critics. Oh yes, I know of all the fine examples of writers who made outstanding critics, but can you guarantee an Olympian detachment when reviewing the book of a critic who slammed yours? Or when writing about the book of a friend of long standing?

The few good critics show what a huge contribution honest and informed criticism can make to the future work of writers. They know who they are. Bless them.

Family problems of the creative artist A writer has a pretty good life, being to a large extent his own master. We have already discussed some of the sacrifices he makes for this

---

* You need to be perfectly certain of both the justice of your cause and the unassailability of your evidence before you threaten journalists, no matter how suavely the threat is conveyed, which is why the features fellow, with his line of communication to the paper's money-people, was invited: to explain the facts of life to the literary editor.

freedom, the main ones being the probability of larger earnings in some other profession, the company at work of his fellows, and the security of a pensionable job. The implications of these matters for the professional writer's family life are obvious. What is less obvious is that a writer *because he is a writer* must make some adaptations in his family life.

Alastair Cooke says he decided over thirty years ago that vacations were for other men; it is not so much that writers are necessarily workaholics as that it is impossible for a man to stop working whose work is whatever passes through his mind. The core of ice at the centre of every writer (Graham Greene) isn't a matter of choice but of nature. A life partner who fights it is a loser before the relationship even starts. Successful writers may be compassionate and passionate people, but anyone who expects them to surrender totally to any experience will be disappointed; there is always a part of every writer that stands apart, that is observing and digesting, that is working.

On a more mundane level, the writer who works at home should leave no one, starting with his own family, in any doubt that what he does is work and deserving of the same consideration as the work of those who go somewhere else to do their job. If you don't do this, you will soon find mounting calls on your time for childminding, errands, housekeeping, gardening, public speaking, charitable work, telling jokes to housewives' coffee mornings, an endless panorama of unproductive tasks. People seem to think that you can always do your writing some other time, but once you give in the other time never seems to arrive. Let them know that what a writer does is write.

Good luck!

INDEX